Strange Tales from ~~East Anglia~~

of pirates, parsons and drunken pigs . . .

*The Norwich mail coach crossing Newmarket Heath
during a thunderstorm. See page 14.*

Derek Richings and Roger Rudderham

S.B. Publications

First published in 1998 by S.B. Publications
c/o 19 Grove Road, Seaford, East Sussex BN25 1TP

ISBN 1 85770 167 4

Typset by JEM Lewes
Printed by Island Press, 3 Cradle Hill Industrial Estate
Seaford, East Sussex BN25 3JE
Telephone: (01323) 490222

CONTENTS

Preface 4

Gentlemen of The Road 5

Perils of The Highways 14

The Lord God Made Them All 25

The Way to the Scaffold 39

A Corpse for The Surgeon 52

Kill or Cure 61

Unusual Causes of Death 74

Men of The Cloth 82

Privateers 92

The Search for True Love 102

PREFACE

THE sections in this book cover so many diverse incidents that occurred in East Anglia between the 17th and 19th centuries, and factual tales of several noteworthy people who lived and died in the region during that period, that rather than list events in formal, chronological order we decided to sectionalize the data we collected under specific subject headings, and present occurrences in an easily readable, entertaining form.

Some of the tales are amusing while others reflect the darker side of the region's past, and although certain incidents and names will be familiar to those interested in local history, we hope that we have presented them in the detailed manner they warrant.

Sources of information include old parish registers, newspapers, long out-of-print books and periodicals. We therefore give credit to the known and unknown writers and artists of long ago who recorded what was happening, and happened, in their time.

We also acknowledge the assistance given to us by the Coleman and Rye Library, Norwich; the Cambridgeshire Collection in Cambridge City Library; Suffolk Record Office, Bury St. Edmunds; Saffron Walden Library, and Colchester Library.

Derek Richings
Roger Rudderham
1998

GENTLEMEN OF THE ROAD

A N ACT of Parliament passed in 1555 directed that every parish would be obliged to provide labour for the upkeep of the highways and that all able-bodied householders were to make themselves available for the task four days a year. An officer, the Surveyor of the Highways, was to be elected in each parish to ensure that all work necessary to keep the highways well maintained was carried out by unwilling, unpaid conscripts.

Needless to say, the Act became unpopular, and the heavy work of harrowing, filling in the deep ruts with broken stones and rubble, then levelling, was more often than not neglected, particularly as the magistrates, burdened with more serious offences, were lax in enforcing the Act.

Most roads therefore remained as little more than rough tracks, which were apt to engulf the hastening traveller in clouds of dust during the dry summer months. In winter they either became a quagmire, or so hardened by frost that the deep ruts caused many wagons and coaches to overturn.

To avoid the numerous pools of water and deep ruts in winter, the astute traveller often chose to wander from the main track to tread firmer ground on the most suitable side until more favourable conditions induced him to re-join it. Many of our winding country roads that exist today evolved from these unofficial diversions.

Whatever the condition, roads at the time were used mainly by pedestrians, horse riders, drovers, strings of pack-horses, laden carriers' wagons, and, occasionally, private coaches owned by the gentry.

Coaches were a status symbol of the day and only the wealthy could afford them. To keep up appearances they vied with each other in boasting ownership of the most luxurious model for the conveyance of guests to their parties in as much comfort as possible.

Adverse road conditions apart, an extra hazard that slow-moving coaches and their bejewelled occupants frequently had to face was a sudden hold-up by armed footpads or highwaymen.

One such notorious fellow was Ipswich-born Thomas Wilmot who, after squandering his inheritance, took to highway robbery. He soon made a name for himself along the Colchester–Chelmsford road as a ruthless outlaw who would stop at nothing to relieve terrified coach passengers of their valuables.

On one occasion, when he had difficulty in wrenching a ring from a lady's finger, he cut off the finger complete with ring without any qualms.

Wilmot's reign came to an end when he held up the Duke of Buckingham's coach in April 1670. Irate at being forced to part with 200 guineas, the duke ordered his men to pursue Wilmot across country until they caught him. He gave them a good run until finally he was caught and arrested at Northampton, where he was tried for numerous capital offences, pronounced guilty and hanged.

Some highwaymen formed gangs to better their chances of attack by might of number, but sometimes had less success than a lone raider. When a gang of nine held up three gentlemen and their footmen, who were returning to London from Newmarket on horseback after a profitable day at the Spring races of 1680, they had not reckoned on encountering fierce resistance. The travellers were all armed and fired their pistols without hesitation.

After a brief battle the gang fled, one bleeding from a wound in the neck, and another with a bullet in his back. The only harm their intended victims suffered was to one of the gentlemen who complained of a sore finger caused by firing his pistol.

Although the majority of highway robbers were men, some women were attracted to a life on the road with the prospect of excitement and rich pickings. Margaret Matthews for instance.

Daughter of a Lavenham swordmaker, Margaret grew up to become a skilled and daring swordswoman herself. Quite by chance she met Ipwich-born Thomas Rumbold who, tired of being apprenticed to a bricklayer, had taken up highway robbery.

Thrilled by Rumbold's accounts of his rewarding adventures, Margaret formed a partnership with him, and they succeeded in terrorising the Suffolk and Essex roads together for nearly five years until she decided to retire and live in Norwich on her illicit earnings, dying there of dropsy in 1688.

Rumbold, having no desire to retire, continued his life of crime, evading capture until he was finally caught and hanged at Tyburn in 1689.

Frank Osborne was another villian of note who stalked the Essex roads. Born in Colchester to wealthy parents in 1661, he was later apprenticed to a goldsmith in Lombard Street, London. After serving his term, Frank set up his own business as a goldsmith, but greed and an unhealthy love for the precious metal were to bring about his downfall.

He became addicted to gambling and soon found himself heavily in debt until, business ruined and unable to face the shame of being sent to the debtors' prison, he took to a life of crime on the roads.

His most daring robbery took place on the Harwich–Manningtree road when, accompanied by a companion, he held up the Earl of Albemarle's coach. Apart from being armed himself, the Earl was guarded by two men on horseback, four footmen, the coachman and the postillion. All carried firearms but were unskilled in using them.

Osborne's demands for the Earl to surrender his money and valuables were answered by a fusillade of widely-aimed shots. Undeterred by this poor show of bravado, Osborne and his partner immediately returned the fire with deadly aim. The Earl surrendered and handed over 130 guineas, a gold watch and all his jewellery, then watched as the culprits galloped away, leaving his two footmen and the guards' horses severely wounded.

Osborne's career came to an end in 1690 when, accompanied by two other highway terrorists, and no doubt flushed with a long run of successes, he foolishly held up the heavily guarded coach of a nobleman on Hounslow Heath. Resistance was so fierce that Osborne's companions fled, leaving him surrounded. Having no choice but to surrender, he was taken to Newgate, tried, and hanged on September 12, 1690, at the age of twenty nine.

In spite of regularly dicing with death, some highwaymen could not resist adding a touch of humour, even if somewhat perverted, to their illegal adventures. Such as Ned Bonnett, a notorious rogue who was much feared by travellers on the Cambridgeshire roads in the early 18th century.

At that time the village of Barnwell, on the edge of Cambridge, was noted for its numerous brothel houses, which were established to cater for the sexual needs of wealthy students from the nearby colleges. Rich students not only provided rich pickings for the highwayman, but an encounter with one sometimes put an end to the student's higher education.

On one occasion, a young student, having decided to impress his chosen courtesan by taking her for a carriage ride along the leafy lanes of Barnwell, was shaken out of whatever desires he had in mind when confronted by Ned pointing two pistols at him. Fearful of not being able to pay the young lady for her services, the student refused to part with his money until Ned set about him and snatched the £6 he had in his purse.

Finding nothing else of value, Ned ordered the student and his courtesan to strip naked. He then sat them in the carriage, tied their hands behind their backs, and whipped the horse, which galloped off at speed, pulling the carriage and its helpless passengers towards Cambridge.

The shame of being brought to a halt in a crowded street of the town in such an embarrassing position was but the beginning of the unfortunate couple's problems. The student was expelled from the university for misconduct, and the woman was sentenced to a short term of confinement in the House of Correction.

What happened to them later is unrecorded but, unconcerned, Ned continued to humiliate his victims. After robbing a nobleman and his retinue of their valuables on another occasion, he ordered the gang he had formed to tie them to a tree, but promised to bring his prisoners company as soon as possible. He kept his word within two hours by returning with more victims who were obliged to undergo the same indignity. Twelve men in all were left to free themselves as best they could.

Ned Bonnett was born in Ely to law-abiding parents who apprenticed him to a grocer in Potton, Bedfordshire, after ensuring he had an elementary education. He learned the trade well, married and opened his own grocery business.

A respectable grocer he might have remained had not his shop and adjoining house been inexplicably destroyed by fire shortly afterwards. Unable to pay his debts Ned left his wife and took to the roads, where he and his gang were said to have committed more than 300 robberies.

But like the majority of his contempories, Ned's luck eventually began to run out when, having had his horse shot from beneath him, he decided to continue his trade on foot. Although he was never caught in a raid, one of his associates turned King's Evidence when captured and disclosed his London hideout. Taken unawares, Ned had no choice but to surrender. He was brought to Cambridge for trial and ended up on the gallows at Cambridge Castle on March 28, 1713.

Samuel Gregory and his followers were the most evil collection of villains who terrorised the quiet Essex countryside. Not content with highway robbery, the Gregory Gang, as they came to be known and feared, also raided people's houses during the small hours. The occupants usually gave in to their demands without resistance but an exception was a farmer called Lawrence who, in spite of his ordeal at the hands of the gang in February, 1735, refused to disclose where the family valuables were hidden.

Unaccustomed to stubborn resistence, Gregory pulled down Lawrence's breeches and forced him to sit on the open fire several times, then poured a kettle of boiling water over him and threatened to murder his terrified family unless he complied with demands. Although in agony, Lawrence would not give in and, with an eye on the clock, the gang left with minimal pickings of £10 in cash and some linen.

The pain and indignity the farmer was forced to suffer in his own home, while his helpless family looked on, caused such an outcry that the authorities offered a £50 reward per head for the capture of Gregory and any member of his gang.

The incentive quickly brought results. Within a month several members of the gang had been captured, and Gregory himself was arrested in an alehouse

Officers of the Law in pursuit of Dick Turpin.

in the village of Moulsham, near Chelmsford. Unrepentant, he even mocked the prayers offered on his behalf before he swung on the gallows at Tyburn in June, 1735.

One member of the Gregory Gang who escaped capture after the attack on the Lawrence house was a young novice named Dick Turpin. Born in the Essex village of Hempstead, in 1706, where his father was landlord of The Bell Inn, he was apprenticed to a butcher in Whitechapel at the age of 16. He returned home after leaving the trade, married, and set up his own business in nearby Thaxted, but, disillusioned, joined the Gregory Gang when the business failed.

Far from being the handsome, dashing hero portrayed in romantic novels, Turpin was only five feet tall, and of slight build. His face was severely pitted by the ravages of smallpox, and the carefully-coiffured wig he always wore covered a sparse head of hair. He was also a merciless scoundrel.

Turpin emerged from hiding when the Lawrence affair had died down and teamed up with highwayman Tom King. Together they plundered many farms and became noted for horse-stealing, but were eventually traced to the Red Lion Inn, Whitechapel, where they had stabled a stolen horse.

In the ensuing battle, Turpin accidentally shot King and fled, leaving his helpless partner to face the consequences. But King died of his wound before the hangman could add him to his list of executions.

Meanwhile, Turpin continued his reign of terror alone, and caused so much havoc on the highways and farms that the reward for his capture was increased to £200. With such a huge price on his head, and unable to trust anyone, he decided to quit East Anglia and head north.

There have been many fictitious accounts of his legendary ride to York, but, while it is true that he did journey there, a lesser known fact is that he changed his name to Palmer and became a horse-dealer. Where the horses came from is another matter, for Dick Palmer, alias Turpin, was soon arrested and hanged for horse-stealing.

In those days courts sometimes ordered a gibbet to be erected near the place where the capital offence was committed, and that the lifeless body of the criminal be left hanging there in chains as a deterrent to other like-minded rogues. Gibbets with rotting bodies swinging from them soon became such a common sight along roads all over the country that they seemed to have the opposite effect on highwaymen, many of whom were daring, adventurous young men who, unable to find any other way of escaping a life of poverty, turned to crime. Success quickly hardened them and they thought of death on the gallows as a far more heroic end than slowly starving in a hovel.

One of the most famous gibbets, a replica of which still stands, was erected on the old North Road near the village of Caxton. Gatwood, a young high-wayman who was sentenced to death for robbing the Royal Mail postboy in 1750, was left hanging from the original Caxton gibbet for nearly four years until the rusting screws supporting the crossbeam gave way on a windy night.

It is said that Gatwood's mother gathered the fallen remains of her wayward son and buried them in the cellar of her inn.

Many highwaymen were never caught and remained anonymous. Some of these were part-timers who occasionally took to the road at night to supplement an inadequate income. They had their successes but generally lacked the skill and cold-blooded nerve of the daylight robbers.

Victims' descriptions of unknown robbers did little to help identify them; 'He was visibly nervous,' said one passenger of the man who held up the Norwich coach near Romford in January 1769. 'Yes,' another agreed, 'his hand was trembling as he held the pistol.' Nervous or not, the unknown attacker managed to relieve them of £3 12s before he fled into obscurity.

Other scoundrels thought up and applied devious means to waylay travellers. James Wilson, for instance, may well have been a frustrated actor. His favourite ploy was to dress as a gamekeeper and stroll nonchalantly along the roads between Brandon and Bury St Edmunds with a loaded shotgun resting on his shoulder when unsuspecting victims drew near.

Gamekeepers were a common enough sight and usually attracted little attention but, partnered by Thomas Kersey, who hid behind the hedgerow ready to pounce, Wilson surprised and robbed many a traveller until he and Kersey were apprehended and brought to trial at the Bury Assizes in March 1760.

Ironically, Wilson, who had thought up the idea, was found not guilty and was acquitted, but Kersey was sentenced to death on the one charge of lurking behind the hedgerow, pouncing on a Mr Parker of Thornham and robbing him of 10 guineas. His appeal for a reprieve was turned down and he was hanged on April 12, 1760. What happened to fake gamekeeper James Wilson thereafter is unrecorded.

By the late 18th century many of the main roads in East Anglia had been taken over by Turnpike Trusts, which ensured they were kept in better repair. Travel times between towns therefore became much faster and the number and frequency of stage coach services steadily increased. Most stage coaches carried armed guards, and attempting to rob one became a risky business for the highwayman.

Nevertheless, some, perhaps driven by desperation, continued to take risks, even though they knew the odds were stacked against them. Many were killed when they attacked, or managed to escape seriously wounded, never to be heard of again.

John Walker was a known robber who met his end when he held up the Norwich coach on a lonely stretch of Newmarket Heath early one morning in January 1776. He ignored warnings that he would be shot if he approached the coach and received a bullet in the body.

The coach immediately moved on to Newmarket, where riders were instructed to search for him. They found him crawling on his hands and knees near the spot where he had held up the coach, but he died of his wound before they could convey him to Newmarket. Ironically, the only weapon he was carrying was an iron candlestick.

Some highwaymen thought the risks of holding up heavily-armed stage coaches were much too great, and turned to robbing easier targets, such as the newly-established turnpike toll gates.

John Flower, the toll collector at the Red Lodge gate, near Newmarket, was called out to open the gates at about nine o'clock in the evening on September 21, 1776. Accustomed to being called out at all hours, he dutifully opened his door to comply, but was confronted by a masked highwayman brandishing a pistol and demanding the toll money.

Before Flower had chance to recover from the shock, he was wounded in the neck when the highwayman's pistol accidently fired, much to the surprise of the highwayman. Nevertheless, he ignored Flower's plight, entered the house, forced the terrified Mrs Flower to hand over the money, and fled.

John Flower was later conveyed to Mildenhall, where a doctor successfully removed the pistol ball from his neck.

John Newman, the toll collector at Hutton, Essex, was not so fortunate when he was confronted by a vicious highwayman late at night on October 28, 1782. Not satisfied with shooting and wounding Newman as soon as he opened the door, the highwayman beat him senseless before entering the house and taking not only the toll money, but also many of Newman's personal valuables, then fled.

Newman died from his extensive wounds a few days after the attack, but in spite of the Turnpike Trust offering a reward of £100 for information leading to the apprehension of the villain, he was never caught.

Joseph Beeton in the condemned cell of King's Lynn gaol.

Before the network of mail coaches covered the majority of main towns in East Anglia, the mail was carried by a lone postboy on horseback. The name was a misnomer as postboys were usually old men, who were tempting prey for highwaymen; for they often carried considerable amounts of money.

The postboy who left King's Lynn to connect with the Wisbech mail coach one Saturday night in October 1782 had no choice but to hand over the mailbags to the highwayman who brought him to an abrupt halt en route.

As the bags contained cash and exchange bills in excess of £1,000, no effort was spared to find the villain, and he was soon named by an informant, no doubt encouraged by a substantial reward, as Joseph Beeton, who was quickly traced and apprehended.

But Beeton was not one to resign himself to defeat and pay the inevitable penalty for his crime. He escaped from Lynn gaol and took lodgings at an inn in Castle Acre. He might have remained free, but the landlord became suspicious and notified the authorities, who sent armed guards to transport him back to gaol, where he was secured in leg irons.

Beeton was pronounced guilty and sentenced to death at Lynn Quarter Sessions in January 1783. The trial lasted six hours and drew considerable attention from the public whose sympathies were with the condemned young man. A crowd of more than 5,000 people gathered near the South Gate to witness the execution, which took place at 11 o'clock following prayers offered by two clergymen and hymns rendered by St Margaret's Church choir.

Unimpressed by the ceremony, Beeton threw himself off the cart and plunged downwards immediately the rope was placed round his neck, thus denying the hangman the satisfaction of ending his life. Beeton's body was later covered in pitch and hung in chains from a gibbet on the Saddlebow Road, close to the spot where he had committed his crime.

Although the highwayman's cry of 'Stand and deliver' was seldom heard after 1800, robberies continued, albeit surreptitiously, for the thieves became more cunning. The luggage of passengers on coaches would mysteriously disappear and the odd mailbag would go missing.

Perhaps the greatest mail coach robbery in the region, if not in the entire country, was that of the London-Ipswich coach on the night of September 9, 1822. One of the four inside passengers was a clerk employed by the bank of Alexander & Company, whose mission was to deliver a sealed box containing £30,000 of the bank's own printed ten, five and one pound notes to its Ipswich branch. The clerk kept the box beside him in the coach and left it only twice for refreshments after making sure the coach door remained open so that he could keep an eye on the box all the time.

When the coach arrived in Ipswich the next day the box was discovered to have been forced opened and emptied during the journey. The mystery was never solved, in spite of the bank offering a reward of £5,000 for information.

To minimise their loss, Alexander & Company issued new notes printed in red and gave notice in the press that the public should refuse to accept any of their notes printed in black. Other banks were quick to take every precaution possible against highway robbery.

The chances of a highwayman surviving an attack on a stage coach, a mail coach, or even a lone armed traveller, became so slender that their lengthy reign of terror came to an end well before the mid-19th century.

Fiction usually portrays highwaymen as dashing, romantic figures. In reality the majority were cold-blooded, merciless scoundrels who thought nothing of maiming or killing anyone who refused to meet their demands.

Gentlemen of the Road, as they were often referred to in their heyday, is perhaps the most inappropriate misnomer ever applied to a particular class of ruthless villains in the history of crime.

PERILS OF THE HIGHWAYS

THE mounted highwayman, lurking ready to pounce, has often been portrayed as the only hazard the road traveller in earlier centuries might suddenly have to face, but there were many more.

Roads were then little more than rough-hewn tracks, linking town to town by the shortest possible route, but to journey along even the best of these was generally a perilous and sometimes fatal adventure for the unfortunate traveller. Nevertheless, regular transport services were set up between towns, firstly by operators of huge carrier's wagons which, although loaded with merchandise, could also accommodate up to twenty passengers.

The cumbersome wagons were pulled by teams of eight or ten horses and could cover a maximum of only twelve miles a day in the most favourable conditions. Passengers were crowded in between loosely packed cargo, but were obliged to pay a high fare for the ride in spite of their discomfort and the risk of injury, or even death.

Martha Warde, for example, having secured a position as a maid in Saffron Walden, was laid to rest in the churchyard as soon as she arrived, dead, in such a wagon on May 24, 1611, after setting off from her home town of Chelmsford alive and well. The particular wagon she boarded was heavily laden with bundles of linen, which shifted as the lumbering vehicle rolled and jolted its way along the uneven road, until part of the cargo fell upon her. Trapped and unable to move or cry for help, Martha suffocated to death. This and similar incidents caused many travellers to choose to walk beside the wagon as best they could and pay for only their baggage to be carried inside.

Carriage of goods by wagon remained the main means of transporting merchandise until the advent of canals and, later, the railways, and the roads became even more perilous as the number of carriers increased, the huge wheels of their heavy wagons almost continually churning up the already uneven surface. Accidents and breakdowns occurred frequently, but not all of them were caused by road conditions.

Although drink-driving was not an offence in those days, John Crowson had sense enough to realize that he was incapable of driving his wagon when he staggered from an inn in Wansford at seven o'clock one evening in

October 1809 with a belly full of ale. But sense must have left him when he entrusted an eleven year-old boy to drive the wagon while he settled down to sleep in the back.

Whether the inexperienced young driver would have completed the journey to London safely will never be known, because he, too, fell asleep as the horses instinctively continued to plod along the familiar route until, just before Water Newton bridge, they lost direction and pulled the wagon down a steep embankment. Startled from his sleep, the boy managed to jump clear and escape from the wagon without harm before it overturned, but Crowson was crushed to death by the loosened load of heavy casks.

But whatever care they took, drivers could not foresee the unexpected happening, like William Nelson from London, who decided to walk beside his team of horses as they pulled the wagon over a bridge near Alconbury in May 1816. The horses took fright when the Boston stagecoach suddenly appeared on the bridge and came speeding towards them. They drew the wagon closer and closer to the bridge wall, inadvertently crushing their helpless driver against the wall, then came to a halt as the Boston coach thundered past, the occupants unaware of what had happened.

Another coach halted at the scene shortly afterwards, and the severely injured Nelson was taken to the Brampton Hut public house where a Mrs Travel, the landlady, refused to take him in for attention in spite of pleas from the coach driver and passengers. Nelson was therefore conveyed several miles further to Buckden, but died from his injuries on the way. The owners of Nelson's wagon held Mrs Travel responsible for his death and took court action against her, which resulted in her agreeing to pay £25 compensation to Nelson's bereaved family.

Even the fastest travel speed in the early 19th century would be classed as a snail's pace today, but over-cautious drivers caused irritation to anyone stuck behind them on a narrow road as they sometimes do now. Perhaps the slowest driver on record at that time was Adam Burrell, who regularly drove a wagon from Litcham to King's Lynn, a distance of about fifteen miles. The one-way journey always took him six to seven hours to complete and earned him the nickname of 'Adam Slow'.

What could only be classed as an Act of God caused a disastrous end to a wagon owned by Betts and Bury of Ipswich as it rumbled along a road near Colchester during a thunderstorm in 1820. Struck by lightning, its cargo of gunpowder ignited, blowing wagon, driver and horses to smithereens. No-one ever determined if there were passengers on board.

An alternative means of passenger travel in the late 17th century was by public stage coach. The first regular service on record between Norwich and

London began in 1681. The journey took two to three days, and the means of conveyance initially earned little favour from the suspicious public, who generally thought it to be a health risk.

As one anonymous scribe put it: '. . . sitting all day in Summer time stifled with heat and choked with dust, or starving and freezing with cold or choked with filthy fogs in Winter . . . fellow passengers oft-times sick, ancient and diseased persons, the travellers are many times poisoned by their nasty scents.'

Such complaints failed to deter the operators from introducing a second coach, named the Confatharrat – a 17th century spelling of confederate – to extend their service between Norwich and London. Consequently, in spite of long and tortuous journeys in unsprung coaches, passengers soon came to accept this means of travel as other operators introduced regular services from place to place along ill-kept roads, which were far from suitable to cope with a steady increase in the flow of traffic.

Many roads were badly in need of improvements, and so a system to finance repairs and provide maintainence was introduced by Parliament. The first Turnpike Trust was granted by Act of Parliament in 1663 to maintain a stretch of the Great North Road through Cambridgeshire. Essex introduced its first turnpike in 1695 and Norfolk followed shortly afterwards. By the 18th century the turnpike system had spread throughout the country, and most major towns and cities were linked by well-maintained roads.

Coach operators vied with each other to attract passengers, naming and elaborately colouring their 'well-sprung' coaches, and claimimg the most comfortable rides and the fastest travel times. In 1762 a stage coach company maintained that its vehicle, the Norwich Machine, could make the journey to London in a day and a half, but it was quickly upstaged by a rival company stating that its coach, The Flying Machine, did it in a day.

Whatever boasts companies made, travel by stage coach was anything but comfortable and, as more and more operators set up and introduced regular services with an emphasis on time taken, it became more dangerous.

Accidents occurred frequently, particularly at blackspots, one of which was the narrow bridge over the River Yar at Cringleford, where a turnpike gate had been fixed to the bridge wall. On a Saturday evening in September 1845, a fore wheel of the Newmarket mail coach caught the end of the gate and shattered, throwing the coach on its side. The startled horses broke loose, but the coachman held on to the reins and was dragged fifty yards along the ground before he managed to bring them to a halt. All the passengers were injured, some severely.

Turnpike gates were often the cause of accidents. A wheel of the Magnet coach caught the post of the Eldon Gate, near Thetford, when it was returning to Norwich on October 25, 1825. Most of the passengers were fortunate to escape with only minor cuts and bruises as the coach overturned, with the exception of a woman who was thrown from her outside seat and ended up crushed to death beneath the coach.

The horses pulling the Regulator coach on a journey to London from Holt on May 7, 1833, must have decided there was no need for them to stand waiting when the driver left them unattended to call at Guist post office. The turnpike gate a little way ahead was wide open at the time, but the gatekeeper's maidservant ran and closed it when she saw the driverless coach on the move.

Once in motion without supervision, the horses had no intention of stopping, and unsuccessfully attempted to jump the gate. They crashed into it and were severely injured by the splintering wood. Although the coach sustained damage it remained upright, and the badly shaken passengers were able to clamber out physically unharmed.

Runaway horses were a hazard travellers by coach often had to endure. A notable incident occurred at the King's Arms in Burgh. The coachman, having business to conduct at the inn, entrusted the horses to a young boy during his absence, but the restless animals were anxious to move on and the bewildered boy let go of the reins when they suddenly started off.

The coach had gone about a mile at increasing speed before the passengers realized that it was driverless, and a tragic ending would undoubtedly have resulted had it not been for a passenger from Norwich, whose clear-thinking and bravery were much talked about afterwards. Calming his terrified fellow passengers, he clambered through a side window, heaved himself on to the roof of the coach and crawled into the driver's box. He had difficulty in reaching the reins, which had fallen over the splinter bar, but eventually managed to gather them and gain control of the horses, bringing the coach to a surprisingly smooth halt.

Apart from the many dangers and discomforts coach passengers were likely to encounter on a journey, the smells emanating from certain types of cargo carried could make it a most unpleasant experience. A new coach named the Lynn Union began a service from King's Lynn to London in 1809, departing every other afternoon and travelling through the night to arrive in London the following morning. Although night travel was undoubtedly considered more hazardous than journeying in daylight, it was the baskets of shrimps the Lynn Union regularly carried that put people off using it. On hot summer nights the stench must have been nauseating.

Passenger business gradually declined until, in 1811, the owners of the Lynn Union were obliged to cease carrying the offensive shrimps on their coaches.

They also introduced a daytime service to London, with more staging posts in an endeavour to attract patrons back.

Complaints to coach owners were numerous and varied, but few were made about the drivers, some of whom became renowned for their characteristic traits as well as their driving skills. The most popular driver of the Lynn Union was Thomas Cross. He was also a part-owner of the company and became well-respected for his sobriety and safe driving.

In his autobiography Cross recounts an incident that could well have been scripted for a farce, but which, to the misfortune of the only victim, actually happened. It was customary for the up and down coaches on the London to King's Lynn run to meet at Trumpington and change drivers. On one such occasion, after exchanging waybills, Thomas mounted his coach, unaware of how close the previous driver had parked it to the gutter. When he drove off, a wheel caught in a grating, causing the coach to tilt towards a cottage.

Unfortunately, or perhaps fortunately, for a woman seated on the top of the coach, the upper window of the cottage was wide open. The sudden jolt caused her to lose her grip on the handrail of the coach and plunge headlong through the cottage window into a large washtub.

Richard Vaughan, driver of the Cambridge Telegraph stage coach.

Courtesy of the Cambridgeshire Collection.

Even the most serious onlooker must have had difficulty in stifling his laughter when she appeared in the cottage doorway shortly afterwards, dripping wet and covered in soapsuds, but otherwise unharmed.

Completely the opposite in temperament to Thomas Cross, Richard 'Dick' Vaughan, a driver of the Cambridge Telegraph coach, took to drink early in life and acquired a reputation for his erratic and reckless driving. He was nevertheless idolized by the boisterous, sport-loving clan of Cambridge University undergraduates, who nicknamed him Hellfire Dick and encouraged him to drive at maximum speed.

But heavy drinking brought about his untimely end. One night in 1816 when he was returning home in his gig after over-imbibing at a country inn, he ran off the road at breakneck speed, crashed, and was killed instantly. He was

18

buried in Puckeridge churchyard, where his plain marble tombstone is said to have been inscribed with just: *ALAS! POOR DICK.*

Driving a stagecoach was a dangerous occupation and many drivers were killed in the numerous accidents which occurred. These were rarely caused by reckless driving, but by a variety of unfortunate incidents, such as a breaking axle, a detached wheel, the skid chain or traces suddenly snapping, a horse stumbling on a loose stone or losing its footing in a hole, and bad weather.

On the evening of February 25, 1833, the Lynn–Newmarket mail coach slid into a deep drain and toppled over when it was overtaking a slow moving carrier's cart on a narrow road near Methwold. The coachman, named Booty, was crushed to death beneath one of the horses as it fell upon him. Mercifully, all the passengers escaped serious injury.

Drivers of the Lynn mail coach over the years seemed particularly prone to disaster. On January 14, 1842, a heavy fall of snow had completely covered the road between Melbourn and Royston. Driver Simpson carried on regardless, but veered off the hidden track and was killed instantly as the coach toppled over and fell upon him. Once again, the passeners were fortunate to escape serious injury.

Adverse weather conditions did not deter coach companies from operating their scheduled services, and the drivers were obliged to set off irrespective of the unforeseen hazards they faced. During the second week of May, 1824, the rainfall was exceptionally heavy and continuous. Rivers overflowed and flooded the roads. Travel conditions became perilous, but coaches continued journeying along their regular but unrecognisable routes.

The Norwich mail coach, which was following close behind The Magnet, managed to halt a few yards short of the bridge at Chesterford before it collapsed, but was rapidly surrounded by the encroaching flood water, which came up to the horses' bellies. Somehow the driver and guard succeeded in turning the horses and coach around and pulled away to safety before the land beneath them also gave way, thus avoiding a major tragedy.

A serious accident occurred near the White Hart Inn, Scole, on February 15, 1821, owing to reckless driving by the driver of The Yarmouth Star, which was on a scheduled journey to London. When he saw a rival coach from Norwich approaching the inn from another direction, the Star's driver became determined to reach the inn first and whipped the horses into a furious pace, much to the alarm of the passengers, who pleaded with him to slow down.

Heedless of their concern, he turned a corner at the same speed and the coach toppled over. A woman passenger suffered a dislocated shoulder, and a man from Leeds, named Samuel Batterfield, sustained serious back injuries, from which he died in agony two months later.

The Norwich mail coach crossing Newmarket Heath during a thunderstorm on its way to London. Courtesy of The Cambridgeshire Collection.

The driver suffered a fractured skull, but was faced with further problems. Samuel Batterfield's employers brought an action against the proprietors of the Star, demanding compensation for 'the loss of their servant through the negligence and furious driving of the coachman'.

Batterfield's employers won the case and were awarded £100 damages, but whether a portion of the award went to his wife and eight children is unrecorded.

Rivalry between coach companies to provide greater comfort and faster journey times to attract custom was fierce. Drivers of rival coaches plying the same route competed to be the first to arrive at a destination. One of the most noteworthy cases recorded of drivers racing against each other occurred on December 30, 1822 when The Norwich Times and The Norwich Day coaches both left London at 5.30am. The Times was driven by John Thorogood, who not only had the reputation of being a crack coach driver but was also a proprietor of the coach company.

The route from London to Norwich was then a distance of 116 miles, and both coaches raced along at breakneck speed, neither stopping to change horses or to pick up or drop passengers over the last twenty five miles. In spite of

20

Thorogood's reputation, the Day was first to arrive in Norwich at 4.45pm, ten minutes ahead of the Times, the driver of the Day setting up a new record of eleven hours, fifteen minutes.

Two rival Cambridge drivers found themselves in court for racing against each other on a return journey from London in 1821, after being reported to the magistrates by a disgruntled passenger. From information given, the magistrates established that the coaches had been travelling at a reckless speed of at least 20 miles per hour, but Joe Walton, the driver of the inappropriatly named Safety coach, was acquitted because he had kept to the right side of the road, and was not seen to whip his horses.

His competitor, driver of the Tally Ho coach, was perhaps unjustly fined the sum of eight guineas, for Joe Walton was the most famous driver on the Cambridge–London route at the time and probably had some influence in the right quarters. Walton was a tall, well-built man who had a short temper and a dislike of women, but was greatly admired as an excellent coachman

Three old Cambridge coachmen – Joe Walton, driver of The Star of Cambridge, in the centre.
Courtesy of The Cambridgeshire Collection.

whose driving skills were second to none. Blocked roads never prevented him from completing a journey. He would divert the coach across fields and drive through hedgerows, and let nothing stop him from keeping to his timetable.

If for some reason he fell behind time, he was wont to drive past passengers waiting to be picked up rather than lose more time at an official halt. Persuading him to stop at an unofficial halt was almost impossible, but a passenger whose hat blew off on one occasion managed it. When Joe refused to stop for him to walk back and retrieve his hat, he lost his temper and knocked Joe's hat off. Swearing under his breath, Joe brought the coach to a halt, and both he and the passenger trudged back to search for their hats.

As skilled a coachman as he was, Joe Walton did not remain accident free, and he upset a coach on more than one occasion. When he was driving The Star of Cambridge on a return journey from London in November 1828, he suddenly increased the pace in an endeavour to catch up with The Defiance coach, which was a short distance ahead.

After changing horses at Buntingford, he caught up with The Defiance and tried to overtake it, but one of his horses, dazzled by the rear lamps of The Defiance, shied, then ran up a bank at the side of the road. The Star toppled over, and Walton and an outside passenger were thrown to the ground. Walton's ankle was dislocated, Mr Bird, a proprietor of the coach, suffered a severely bruised face and three passengers received minor injuries.

Six years later, on a return journey from London, Walton handed the reins of The Star to Sir Vincent Cotton, a baronet, who fancied himself as a skilled coach driver. The honourable gentleman might have remained more respected had he kept his fancies to himself, for he lost control of the horses when descending Reed Mill Hill, near Royston, and the coach rolled over. An outside passenger suffered a fractured leg, and Joe Walton a sprain to the same ankle that was dislocated in the earlier Buntingford accident.

Only a week later, the ill-fated Star was involved in another accident near Buntingford. This time, in the absence of the injured Walton, it was being driven by Valentine Carter, who had no chance of avoiding a collision with a runaway carrier's wagon. Amazingly nobody was injured in the crash, and the passengers were so impressed with the way Carter handled the incident that they jointly wrote a letter, which was published in the local press, supporting his claim that he was in no way to blame for the accident.

Carter later took up the reins of The Rocket coach and was greatly admired, not just as a coachman, but also as a respected citizen, for it was said that 'a more upright, truthful and honourable man never lived'.

The Norwich Day coach was involved in a gruesome accident on its return from London on a foggy evening in February 1843 whilst attempting to overtake a slow-moving brewer's dray at Tasburgh. Thomas Wiggins, the driver of the Day, misjudged the width of the road and and was thrown head first from his seat into a tree as the coach caught the side of the dray, overturned, and plunged down a steep bank at the side of the road.

The guard, a young man named William Elvis, was also thrown head first on to the stump of a tree and was killed instantly. Mr Scott, a passenger, was helplessly trapped between the upturned coach and a tree, which had to be cut down before he could be extricated.

The severely injured Wiggins was conveyed to The Bird in Hand, a nearby inn in Tasburgh, where he hovered between life and death for several days.

The Lynn Union stage coach preparing to leave London.
Courtesy of The Cambridgeshire Collection.

Although he gradually recovered from the ordeal, he never regained full health, and died on April 24, 1844 at the age of thirty eight.

On May 1, 1844, only a week after the death of coachman Wiggins, the first stretch of railway in the region opened for business. This was the twenty and a half mile length of track between Yarmouth and Norwich. George Stephenson, builder of the famous Rocket locomotive, was appointed chairman of the company, and his son, Robert, the engineer.

The momentous occasion signalled the certain demise of the coaching era as the railway network gradually spread throughout East Anglia, linking Norwich to Brandon, Brandon to Ely, Ely to Cambridge, and Cambridge to London. Soon most major towns were linked to lines running to London.

One by one the stage coach companies went out of business as the railway rapidly captured their custom. One of the last coaches to struggle against such powerful competition was the old Lynn Union, whose driver, Thomas Cross, wrote this sad account of his last days at the reins of his beloved coach:

'On approaching the inn, not a solitary person did I see. The dingy, half-washed coach stood by itself outside the gates, like a deserted ship; inside there was a dim, dirty place set aside for the office . . . in it glimmered one poor mutton candle, stuck on a piece of rusty tin that had served the ostler for a candlestick for years . . . by its light I entered and could just perceive a lantern-jawed, melancholy looking man – whose visage indicated, indeed seemed to already anticipate, the fate that awaited both him and me – leaning with his head upon his hands, inert and heedless, as must men who have nothing to do. This was the porter. On the other side of the counter, behind an old worm-eaten desk, sat the book-keeper. The usual salutation having passed between us, I took from the desk a long sheet of white paper, the waybill, which, with the exception of the heading, was unsullied – not the name of a passenger or parcel was written thereon.'

Cross's recollection of that stop probably sums up the sunset of the most romantic and perilous means of public transport better than anything else ever written – but what happened to all the daring coachmen who were 'steamed out' of a job?

Well, Tom Cross secured a position with the Paving Commissioners in Cambridge, where he lived. Joe Walton was engaged by a Cambridge bank, Messrs Fosters. The job entailed him journeying to London once a week – by train. Joe would never sit with his back to the 'iron-horse' as some called it, and must have been the only passenger who was delighted when the train arrived late. The majority of redundant coachmen seem to have faded into obscurity to live out their lives with only memories of their adventurous years on the road.

THE LORD GOD MADE THEM ALL

L EGEND has it that the British Isles, known as Albion by the Romans, were once inhabited by a race of giants, two of whom, named Gog and Magog, are supposedly buried on the Gogmagog hills south of Cambridge.

Figures of the two giants, carved in the hills hundreds of years ago, were once clearly visible for miles around, but were obscured by undergrowth by the early 18th century.

Perhaps the Fen giant Tom Hickathrift was descended from this race of giants. Tom was supposed to have been born near Wisbech in the 11th century, and many tales of his exploits are still told in the Cambridgeshire and Norfolk Fens. Although his reputed grave can be seen in the churchyard of Tilney All Saints, he probably never exsisted and can be relegated to legend and folklore.

The adventures of old Tom may well have been familiar to Susan Carter of Histon when she gave birth to her second son in 1801. She and husband James had no reason to think that the baby would grow to become a giant. They named him Moses, and had their time cut out in frequently finding clothes that would fit him during the course of his rapid physical development. When he reached manhood, Moses stood 7ft tall and weighed 23st.

Moses lived in Histon all his life, and earned a living as a market gardener. He was so strong that he never made use of a horse to cart his vegetables to Cambridge and Ely markets, but pulled the conveyance himself.

He became a much-loved character, a gentle giant easily recognisable wherever he went in his stovepipe hat and huge hobnail boots. He never married, but lived alone in a hut built with clay bricks, where he made daily use of a nearby pond for bathing and washing his clothes, whatever the weather – the kitchen copper being exclusively reserved for boiling his huge meals, such as beef stew and dumplings. Moses died in 1860 and was buried in Histon churchyard.

But as tall as he was, Moses would have had to look up to James Toller had they been contemporaries. James was born in 1798 to parents of average stature who lived in Eynesbury, near St Neots. As a child, James had only a moderate appetite and was of slender build, but he continued to grow after his tenth birthday when he had reached 5ft 5in.

He must have caused some embarrassment to his parents as a youth because he was often reported as swinging on the signboards of public houses and peering in bedroom windows as he wended his way through the streets of Eynesbury.

In 1815 James took part in a London exhibition, where he was billed as The Young English Giant, and was presented to Tsar Alexander I of Russia when the Tsar visited the exhibition. The young giant then exhibited himself at Kirby's Wonderful Museum, London, in the contrasting company of a Dutch dwarf named Simon Paap, who stood only 28in high.

By the time he was eighteen, James was 8ft 1fiin tall and, perhaps tired of exhibiting himself, enlisted in the army. But the physical demands of military life proved too much for him. His health deteriorated and he was discharged after only a short taste of service life. He returned to Eynesbury to live with his mother in a cottage near the rectory, and became a recluse as his health continued to decline. The rector encouraged him to exercise in the rectory gardens and often took him for a countryside carriage drive, but to no avail. James died on February 4, 1818, at just twenty. He was then 8ft 6in tall and possibly still growing.

Word spread that medical researchers had offered large sums of money for his body, and he was buried beneath the aisle of Eynesbury church to foil the bodysnatchers.

James Toller, the Eynesbury Giant, who grew to 8ft 6in tall.

Robert Hales, who was born in the village of Somerton, near Great Yarmouth, in 1820, became even more of a celebrity than James Toller. Both his parents were more than 6ft tall, but were overtaken in height by Robert, and his sister, Mary. Robert not only grew to 7ft 2in, but tipped the scales at 33st. He measured 62in round the chest and 64in round the waist. He began his working life as a wherryman, but when he was approached by a showman named Lasky in 1840 he soon realized he could earn much more by exhibiting himself as a freak at the numerous fairgrounds .

Lasky was even more impressed when he met Robert's sister Mary, who was also over 7ft tall, and he persuaded the two of them to appear first at Camberwell fair, where they were billed as The Giant and Giantess from

Norfolk. To encourage people to visit the booth, apart from curiosity, Lasky announced that he would pay 100 guineas to any woman who physically equalled Mary Hales. The challenge drew the crowds but was never taken up.

After spending a few years exhibiting themselves at fairs, Robert and Mary went their separate ways. What became of Mary is not known, but Robert set sail for America in 1848 to join Barnum and Bailey's Circus. He remained in their employ for two years, then returned to England to take over a tavern in Drury Lane. But, despite many people visiting expressly to see him, the business did not pay. During his stay in London he was presented to Queen Victoria and Prince Albert, who gave him a gold watch and chain.

Falling trade at the tavern forced him to return to the fairs for a few years until his health deteriorated and his only means of earning a meagre living was by selling his life story in the streets of Norwich. In 1864 he died of consumption and was buried in Somerton churchyard.

John Coan, who was born at Twitshall, Norfolk, in 1728, stopped growing when he was a young child. Although perfectly formed he stood just 38in tall and weighed only 34lb at the age of twenty two. Like many other human curiosities, he found he could best earn a living on the fairgrounds, but not by just exhibiting himself, for John was also a song and dance artiste, known as the Norfolk Pigmy. Eventually he was summoned to appear before the Dowager Princess of Wales and the Prince of Wales, and entertained them for two hours. The royal pair were so delighted with his performance that they presented him with what was reported to be 'a handsome present', and probably enthused about his talents in royal circles as he was presented to King George II later the same year.

During the last years of his life, Coan was employed by a showman named Pinchbeck to entertain the customers at a tavern he owned in Chelsea Fields. Pinchbeck astutely re-named the place The Dwarf's Tavern, and many visitors came to see the little fellow, and hear him sing humorous songs and dance on the table tops. But long hours of performing practically non-stop nearly every night soon exhausted the frail entertainer and his health rapidly declined. He died at the tavern on March 16, 1764.

In an attempt to encourage visitors to continue patronising the tavern, Pinchbeck installed a waxwork model of John Coan, but the public soon decided that a motionless effigy was a poor substitute for a jovial live pigmy.

Kelham Whitelamb was another East Anglian midget who exhibited himself at fairs. He was born in 1765, although his place of birth has never been established, as both Wisbech and Ipswich are mentioned in conflicting tales.

At twenty two, and described on billboards as 'not quite two feet tall', he certainly attracted the crowds by being transported around in a miniature sedan chair like a tiny king.

Kelham would have been obscured by the shadow of Edward Bright, a native of Maldon, Essex, who became famous for his huge bulk. He weighed 10 stones at the age of twelve, but was very agile, and a skilled rider, which helped him obtain a job as a postboy, delivering mail between Maldon and Chelmsford.

Things might have turned out differently had he stuck to an occupation unconnected with food, but, after a short period of delivering mail Edward was offered an apprenticeship with a local grocer, and he jumped at the opportunity.

Eventually he opened his own grocery shop in Maldon, where he was in his element, stuffing himself with huge meals and drinking at least a gallon of beer every day until he tipped the scales at 42 stones.

*Kelham Whitelamb,
the Wisbech Dwarf.*

Measuring 6ft 11in round the waist and 2ft 2in round each leg Edward, not surprisingly, had difficulty carting his huge bulk around without becoming breathless and exhausted. When his legs became inflamed he was rendered immobile. In 1750 he contracted typhus and died on November 19. A coffin measuring 6ft 7in long, 3ft 6in wide and 3ft deep was especially constucted to accommodate his massive corpse, but no-one had thought how they were going to get it out of the house. The coffin had been sealed when they realized that the doorway was too narrow and the window too small.

After giving the problem considerable thought they demolished a wall of the house and were thus able to haul the coffin on to a heavy wagon outside, to convey it to the church. The final problem of how to lower it into a vault steadily was solved by rigging up a system of ropes and pulleys.

The Maldon parish register states that Edward Bright was 'comely in his person, affable in his temper, a kind husband, a tender father and a valuable friend'. It does not state that he also held the record of being England's fattest person, until Daniel Lambert took the unenviable title from him by an extra

Heavyweight Daniel Lambert, and his grave in the churchyard at Stamford.

ten stones some years later. Lambert was born in Leicester in 1770, and showed no signs of being anything other than a normal, healthy, agile boy until he was twelve years old when he developed a physical disorder and began to gain weight rapidly. At the age of twenty eight he weighed thirty two stones, but continued piling it on. By the time he was thirty six he weighed 52 stones and measured 9ft 4in round the waist.

In 1791 he was appointed gaoler at Leicester prison, but when the prison closed in 1805 he reluctantly agreed to exhibit himself in the London sideshows and took up residence in Piccadilly. Although he earned a reasonable living from the numerous visitors who paid a shilling each to see him, he soon tired of being on show for several hours every day, and returned to Leicester after five months, where he attempted to live in seclusion on the annuity Leicester magistrates settled on him for his past services as gaoler.

He didn't find it easy to manage on the regular but small amount paid and, after struggling for two years, decided to exhibit himself again by touring East Anglia in a specially reinforced coach. Whilst staying in Ipswich for a few days, he was weighed on a Caledonian Balance, which registered 52st 11lb. In June 1809 he resided at the King's Head, Cambridge, for a while before continuing his tour of East Anglia. But when he arrived in Stamford and took up rooms at the Waggon and Horses Inn his tour came to a sudden and unexpected end, for he dropped dead there at 9am on June 21, at the age of thirty nine.

Unfortunately for the landlord of the inn, a wall had to be demolished before Lambert's enormous body could be removed from the premises. It was placed in a huge elm coffin, mounted on wheels, which upwards of twenty men had difficulty lowering into his grave in St Martin's churchyard.

Thomas Wood, a miller of Billericay, Essex, had an insatiable appetite. After surviving the ravages of smallpox during childhood, he took a dislike to fruit and vegetables and would eat only fattening foods. His love of fat meat, suet puddings and cheese gradually developed into a craving, until he was gorging himself on three huge meals of their like every day, washing them down with vast quantities of strong ale and wine.

In 1762, when he was forty three, he weighed 23 stones, and suffered from gout, rheumatism and breathing problems. He sought help from his doctor, who said he could do nothing for him as the reasons for his ill-health were solely due to his gluttony, and he warned Thomas that his health would rapidly worsen if he did not curtail his intake of food and drink.

Fearful for his life, Thomas made a supreme effort and restricted himself to three frugal meals a day and one pint of beer. The resultant loss of weight and improvement in health pleased him so much that he gave up beer altogether and reduced his food intake even further. The desire to attain perfect health and a trim body developed into an obsession. Regular exercises with dumb-bells and a cold bath morning and night were added to his daily routine.

In 1767, dieting solely on puddings made from flour and skimmed milk, he became so thin and haggard that he was known as 'the ghastly miller of Billericay'. Surprisingly, considering all the drastic changes his body had undergone, Thomas Wood lived to the age of 63. He collapsed suddenly and died in 1783.

When he was six years old, Ezekial Law of Fulbourn, Cambridgeshire, developed a craving for water and consistently thirsted for more, no matter how much he drank. After gurgling at least 3figal during the day, he never retired to bed without taking a full 2gal container of water with him so that he could satisfy his insatiable thirst, which persisted throughout the night.

Apart from his abnormality, he is said to have lived a healthy life, eating moderately, and enjoying an occasional tankard of beer. He believed in regular exercise and frequently took long walks in the country, during which he was able to quench his insatiable thirst by drinking from drains, dykes and ponds along his chosen route. He died at the age of forty four on October 3, 1834, but the cause of death was not recorded. A statistician calculated that the water addict had consumed the equivalent of 1,330fi large barrels of water over a period of thirty eight years, but perhaps an equally interesting statistic, albeit more delicate, would be how many hours Ezekial had spent relieving himself in the water closet during those years!

Charley Strickson, a cobbler, who lived in Stanground, Peterborough, had such a dread of gaining weight, that the very sight of a portly person made him shudder. He would even cross the street to avoid an encounter with anyone whom he considered to be overweight. An eccentric dresser, he aways wore a cutaway coat and a pair of shrunken black trousers that left his spindle legs exposed up to his knees. A beaver top hat and low-heel buckle shoes completed his attire, but he was never seen without a flower in his lapel, which he would usually replace during the summer months with a common nettle and inform everyone who questioned why he was wearing it: 'Stroke it the right way, sir, and it won't sting – neither will a Strickson'.

Charley was a good shoemaker whose oddities mattered little to his patrons as long as he kept them well shod. He often claimed that he came from noble stock, but was never challenged to prove it, and died in 1857 at the age of seventy, his sketetal form a warning to others of the bodily ravages of anorexia.

John Brown, a licencee of the Yarmouth Bridge public house in Red Lion Street, Norwich, had no fear of gaining weight but, for some reason, decided that he must keep to a strict diet of dry toast and tea and let nothing else pass his lips. Even so, he must have consumed vast quatities daily because he rapidly increased weight until he tipped the scales at 27st. He could not keep awake for long, and would inconveniently fall asleep in the middle of a conversation, so was confined to bed, where he spent the rest of his days until he died in 1840 at the early age of thirty nine.

Known as the 'Sleeping Beauty of Stapleford', Sarah Carter, the daughter of a Cambridgeshire farmer, contracted typhus in 1827 when she was nursing her bed-ridden father, who was stricken with the disease. Sarah was only fifteen years old when she first became aware that something was wrong with her. Typhus ravaged her body for two years until she fell into a coma and remained in that state for seventeen weeks.

Unexpectedly, she then came out of the coma, but remained weak, lethargic and confined to bed, and swallowed little sustenance except a few sips of water. She remained in this sad condition for the rest of her life, dying in 1855 when she was forty five years old.

Some doctors believed that Sarah's condition was curable, but her mother refused to allow them to experiment with the latest medicines, no doubt believing that her daughter had suffered enough.

The rare condition of prolonged sleep, commonly known as a trance, struck Elizabeth Perkins of Morely, Norfolk, in 1788, when no-one could wake her for eleven days and six hours. She then suddenly roused, but remained drowsy and listless for another week until she again sunk into a peaceful sleep that was to last for the next two years. During this time, she took no nourishment and appeared to be in a state of suspended animation. She died in 1790 without ever waking again.

Prolonged trance-like conditions were not easily distinguishable from death in those days, but although there is no evidence that people so afflicted were conveniently pronounced dead and consigned to the graveyard, medical practitioners were sometimes accused of prematurely declaring a person dead after burial had taken place.

Elizabeth Perkins of Morley, Norfolk, who remained comatose for eleven days.

Groans were reported to have been heard coming from the grave of a newly-buried woman in St Julien's churchyard, Norwich, in June 1819. The woman, a victim of smallpox, had been buried in haste, and suspicion grew as to whether she was actually dead. The body was exhumed by public demand, but it was proved that the woman had died from the ravages of the disease before arrangements were made to have her buried.

No-one questioned whether Squire Holland of Quidenham Hall was actually dead when he was buried after what must have been one of the most bizarre funeral ceremonies on record. Mourners and pall-bearers alike were so drunk that they could hardly stand, but were making the most of the last request of the eccentric squire, a notorious imbiber.

Long before his death he stipulated that when his time came, he was to be carried in his coffin to the churchyard by twelve drunken men when the clock struck midnight. There were plenty of volunteers for the macabre job, but perhaps selection of the coffin-bearers was based on the twelve who were judged to be more drunk than the others. Drunk and practically incapable of walking a straight line without a burden they certainly were, for when they attempted to carry the coffin across a narrow bridge, they stumbled over the low wall and the coffin toppled into the stream below. It was retrieved with difficulty and the funeral proceeded without further mishap, but, the thought of finishing his time on earth soaked in water would have no doubt stretched the Squire's peculiar sense of humour to the limit.

Edward Noakes, a tinker who lived in Hornchurch, Essex, was known for his miserly ways – but he spent an inordinate amount of money on drink. He consumed at least a quart of spirits a day, and his addiction must have hastened his end. But in all other respects he was frugal to the extreme.

He hoarded his money in a tin box, which he kept beneath loose bricks in his kitchen, and left instructions that his funeral should be arranged at minimal cost. The cheapest coffin, tied by cord instead of nailed, was provided and just 2/6d was to be shared between the six men who carried it. So concerned was he about other people's extravagance that he insisted that no-one should wear expensive mourning apparel at his funeral. Consequently, everyone who attended donned the most colourful clothes they could find in their wardrobes, the undertaker being the most conspicuous in a magnificent blue coat and a bright red waistcoat.

Sir Hervey Elwes of Stoke College, near Clare, was another renowned miser, who was reputed to have limited his spendings to a maximum of £100 a year, which included wages he was obliged to pay the three servants in his employ. Wearing clothes that had been left to him by his ancestors (at least fifty years out of fashion) until they were threadbare, he would spend hours on his estate every day stalking partridges, which he captured by net rather then spend money on shot.

Apart from an occasional boiled potato, he ate nothing other than the birds he caught, which he cooked on a fire made from wood gathered from his estate, but he used the wood sparingly, for cooking purposes only. Even during the winter months he attempted to keep warm by walking briskly up and down the corridors of his house instead of lighting fires to heat the place, and he would retire to bed before dark to avoid burning candles.

But Sir Hervey had a shock one night when thieves broke into his house, dragged him out of bed and threatened to shoot him unless he revealed where he kept his hoard of money. Petrified for his life, he disclosed the hiding place, and watched helplessly as the robbers filled their sacks, then fled with his hoard of 27,000 guineas. But that huge amount must have been only part of his accumulated wealth because, when he died in 1763, Sir Hervey left a considerable fortune to his nephew, John Meggot, who had admired his uncle, and lived his life in an equally miserly fashion thereafter.

When the Guardians of The Poor for the parish of Littleport were informed of the dreadful conditions in which an old woman named Tabitha Camm was living in an isolated spot on the edge of the fens, they decided that she should move into the workhouse at Ely after seeing her dilapidated abode themselves. The roof of what had once been a tiny cottage had partially collapsed, the walls were crumbling and the windows had fallen out, but when the Guardians told Tabitha that the place was dangerous and a threat to her life, she stubbornly refused to leave it and told them to mind their own business. The Guardians then attempted to have her declared insane and forcibly removed to a sanitorium, but failed. As a last resort, they had the cottage condemned as unfit for habitation, but Tabitha ignored an order to vacate it and they gave up attempting to get her out and allowed her to live in the shambles of a dwelling for the remainder of her life.

After she died from natural causes in 1898, £400 was discovered stitched inside her stays. If she had not been such a miser she could have spent her days in comfort by either paying someone to keep the cottage in good condition or moving into a respectable property.

William Monson never had any money to hide. Said to be the illegitimate son of a nobleman, he had left his maternal home in Lincolnshire at an early age to join a company of strolling players. After spending several years travelling from place to place and playing minor roles in sketches and plays, William, tired of always being on the move and short of cash, decided to settle in King's Lynn and launch himself as a shoe-black.

He soon became a well-known figure in the town, not necessarily for his business of blacking shoes, but for his entertainment value, for he had a collection of play-script books, many of which he had memorized, and was delighted when clients asked him to enact scenes from a particular play.

Billy Boots, the thespian shoeblack of King's Lynn.

Widely known as Billy Boots, he was of diminutive stature, had a shuffling gait and a high-pitched monotonous voice, but was oblivious to sarcastic and critical comments from his clients, who usually gave him a small tip for his improvised performances.

William also had a passion for the fairer sex and would spruce himself up in a worn scarlet coat to try and impress and win their affections, always without success.

Undeterred, he continued blacking shoes whilst keeping an eye on the gentler sex until the day he died, unmarried, on January 6, 1815 at the age of seventy.

Jemmy Gordon was born into wealth and never worked or wanted for anything during his early years. The son of a wealthy Cambridge landowner, he was given the best education money could buy, studied the classics and law at University, and later gained articles as an attorney. He then set up his own successful practice in the town and seemed to have everything going for him until the day his intended bride jilted him and ran off with an undergraduate.

Jemmy was shattered and took to heavy drinking. He also tried to console himself by starting an affair with a mercenary mistress of low morals, who was soon referred to as the Duchess of Gordon by his friends. She had extravagant tastes, and encouraged him to drink heavily so she could have him at her mercy and make him succumb to her financial demands.

His permanent state of intoxication made would-be clients shun his business, and it was not long before he was penniless, forced to sell his spacious house and move into cheap lodgings. His mistress, of course, had since left him. Jemmy slid into a state of personal neglect. Shabby and dirty, he dressed in cast-off clothing and relied on whatever coins people in the street would toss his way for an income.

His personality change from that of a pleasant, entertaining wit to a vindictive, blaspheming drunk, who paraded around the town spreading scandalous tales about people, soon drew the attention of the authorities. They considered him to be a public nuisance and asked him to leave town. Jemmy somehow made his way to London where he spent most of his time awaiting the arrival of coaches from Cambridge and begging money from the passengers. He became even more of a nuisance in the capital and was often locked up by the police for long periods.

Homesickness eventually overcame him and he wended his way back to Cambridge, where the proprietor of the Hoop Hotel mercifully allowed him to sleep in the loft of the straw chamber. One night, drunk as usual, he misjudged his footing when he was ascending the ladder to the loft, fell heavily and broke his thigh. His incoherent calls for help were either unheard or accepted as drunken ramblings by anyone who passed nearby, and he spent an agonising night on the hard chamber floor, unable to move, until the ostlers arrived the next morning.

Addenbrooke's Hospital refused to admit him when he was conveyed there, because of his filthy state, so he was taken to the workhouse where he remained until he died at the age of sixty three in September, 1825.

When Abraham Cawston told his father, John, a small farmer at Chippenham, near Newmarket, that he had come into a small fortune, John could hardly believe his ears. Abraham explained how he had first become acquainted with an old man named Don Gaspar de Quintilla when journeying to Shrewsbury on the same stagecoach. They engaged in conversation, mainly centred on South American affairs, and although they had not seen eye to eye on several matters, they parted on friendly terms when the coach arrived at Shrewsbury.

Abraham said that he soon forgot about the chance meeting with de Quintilla until he received an invitation to visit the old man in his house several weeks later. He accepted and enjoyed conversing with his host so much that he began visiting him regularly, and the two formed a firm friendship.

De Quintlla had no living relatives, and when he fell ill several months later, he summonded Abraham to his deathbed and told him that he had made him the sole beneficiary of his Will. Apparently he owned estates in Sicily, France and Germany, which were collectively valued at half a million pounds.

Abraham went on to tell his father that the matter was presently in the hands of solicitors in Liverpool and that it would take them several months to sort out de Quintilla's numerous far-flung assets and settle the amount of his inheritance. But inevitably, as news of Abraham's forthcoming fortune spread, bankers and financiers fell over themselves to secure his custom by offering substantial loans without obtaining proof of his story's authenticity.

He took advantage of them all and began to live in a grandiose style on borrowed money, engaging servants, and inviting celebrities to extravagant dinner parties. At one such dinner, a London vintner became suspicious of the wine, which Abraham boasted was produced in Sicily at the de Quintilla vineyards. When he returned to London, the vintner began making enquiries, and discovered that there were no de Quintilla estates in Sicily, France, or Germany. Further investigations revealed that there was no such person as Don Gaspar de Quintilla.

Abraham Cawston had invented the whole story. He had fooled everyone, but disappeared, leaving enormous debts behind him before the law could catch up with him. As far as is known, he was never seen or heard of again.

Many fortunes have been won and lost on the back of a horse at Newmarket races, occasionally not by honest means. In the 18th century, Samuel Chifney, a Norfolk-born jockey, was accused of being dishonest and banned from participating in the sport after Sir Charles Bunbury and other members of the Jockey Club had invesigated allegations that the result of two races Chifney entered, on the same horse, had been fixed.

On October 21, 1791, he had mounted Escape, a horse bred by the Prince of Wales, in a fifty guineas race against three other horses. Escape was firm favourite at odds of 2-1, but was surprisingly beaten. The result might have been forgotten if Chifney had not ridden the same horse again the next day in another race against five horses, two of which had beaten Escape the previous day, at reduced odds of 5-1. Escape was a clear winner, and those who had backed him won a considerable amount of money, including Chifney and the Prince of Wales, neither of whom had placed bets on the previous day's race.

Although Chifney vehemently denied that he had deliberately held Escape back in the first race, he was found guilty. The Prince of Wales, who many suspected of being the instigator of the 'fix', closed his stables at Newmarket to avoid becoming involved in further scandal and was never seen there again.

Samuel Chifney, who was undoubtedly one of the most skilled jockeys of his time, was banned from racing. In his autobiography he boasted that he 'could ride a horse in a better manner than any person known in my time'. Gradually he drifted into debt and was eventually committed to the Fleet Prison, London, where he died in 1807 at the age of fifty three.

Although the integrity of jockeys remained questionable for some time, no-one found reason to suspect Frank Buckle, the son of a Newmarket saddler, who proved himself completely trustworthy in a successful and brilliant career. He won the Derby five times, the 1000 Guineas six times, and the Oaks nine times, setting a record that is unsurpassed to this day. But one race that Buckle never forgot was held at York in 1805 when he was beaten by a woman jockey.

Alicia Meynell, the daughter of a Norwich watchmaker, raced under the name of Mrs T, and made her debut at the age of twenty two at York races on May 25, 1804, before a large gathering of people. Although she rode well her horse tired and she came nowhere in the race, probably finishing to the jeers of the crowd, as a female jockey was generally unheard of in those days.

But a year later, she shocked onlookers. Glamorously attired in a purple cap and jacket, a yellow cotton shirt, embroidered stockings and purple shoes, she rode against Buckle at York and beat him to win by half a neck. In spite of his otherwise magnificent record, Frank was never allowed to forget the day he was beaten by a woman.

The horse-racing world was shocked by the tragic death of champion jockey Fred Archer in 1886. Although he did not have the build of a jockey, Fred stoically fought a weight problem to become the most successful jockey of his day, winning the Derby five times and the 2000 Guineas four times, but not without cost to his health. For thirteen years he stuck rigidly to a diet consisting of half an orange and a measure of hot castor oil for breakfast, and either a sardine or two oysters washed down with champagne for dinner. He also spent several hours a day sweating in a turkish bath.

He had practically wasted away at the age of twenty nine and began to suffer from depression and convulsions, until the afflictions became so severe that he could stand no more. Ironically, he blew his brains out with a silver pistol that had been presented to him for winning the Liverpool Cup.

Some people still claim to have seen his ghost galloping across Newmarket Heath towards the starting post at midnight every year on November 8, the anniversary of his death.

Measures were usually taken in the past in an endeavour to prevent anyone who had committed suicide to come back as an apparition and haunt the living. When Mary Turrell of Harleston was apprehended for drowning her new-born child in a pond in April, 1813, she poisoned herself rather than face the prolonged torment of a trial and possible execution. The coroner returned a verdict of *felo de se* (self murder). On the same evening, her body was buried in the highway after a stake had been driven through her heart. A large crowd witnessed the gruesome ritual.

In 1799 the Ely coroner directed that the body of John Layton, who had hanged himself, was to be buried near Barton pits on the road to Sutton. Later that year, a stone bearing the following inscription was placed near his grave:

> 'All ye that pass by, pray to
> God to preserve and keep you
> from the crime of Self-murder,
> on which occasion this stone
> was erected in memory of John
> Layton, 1799.'

When twenty two-year-old Elizabeth James of Peterborough confessed to her vicar her anguish and disappointment at the dissolution of her marriage, his advice did not console her, as she killed herself with poison shortly afterwards. The coroner returned a verdict of *felo de se*, and Elizabeth's body was buried about a mile from Peterborough on the road to Spalding on a dark night in May, 1811. Six female relatives, dressed in white, took part in the eerie ceremony which was witnessed by a large crowd of people.

John Bolton, a glover from Bungay, became depressed and disillusioned with life in 1731, and decided to cut his throat, but bungled the act and survived. Undeterred, he tried to hang himself, but made such a noise when he was choking to death at the end of an ill-fitting rope that he was discovered and cut down before he could gasp his last breath.

Still determined to end his life, John, a non-swimmer, thought that the surest way to succeed was to drown himself in the river. Choosing a quiet spot where the water was deep, he plunged in, but had failed to notice a group of people sitting nearby, who, seeing him floundering helplessly fully-dressed, immediately came to the rescue and dragged him out. Totally frustrated, John concluded that he was not meant to commit suicide, but what happened to him afterwards, and how and when he died is not known.

THE WAY TO THE SCAFFOLD

UNTIL the Criminal Law Acts were passed by Parliament in the first quarter of the 19th century, 200 offences could lead to capital punishment. The majority of these unlawful activities were petty offences, such as stealing a handkerchief, shop-lifting, shooting a rabbit, and even sacrilige.

However, most criminals who ended their days on the scaffold had committed more serious crimes, such as murder, arson, burglary, forgery, highway robbery, and horse stealing. The age or sex of the criminal sentenced to hang was considered incidental until 1908, when a Special Act was passed abolishing capital punishment for those below sixteen years of age. Until then, younger people were considered solely responsible for their crimes and even tried and sentenced in the same manner as adults.

Apart from hanging, various methods of executing those sentenced to death have been used by the English over the centuries. Burning alive was the usual method of disposing of those condemned for practising witchcraft or heresy, and for women found guilty of civil offences. Sometimes the condemned person was first strangled until he or she was rendered unconscious and less likely to suffer the full horror of being burned alive, which seems a warped way of showing some mercy.

Amy Hutchinson was sentenced to be burned at the stake at Elyon November 7, 1750, for the murder of her husband. The jury reached the decision after hearing how she had married John Hutchinson in a fit of pique after being deserted by her lover who, after promising to marry her, had fled to London, supposedly to find work, swearing that he would soon return. Fed up with waiting, and not even hearing from him, Amy took up with Hutchinson and reluctantly argeed to marry him, although she still yearned for her absent lover who, perhaps unfortunately, returned shortly after the wedding.

Amy's coolness towards Hutchinson, their consant quarrels, and the severe beatings she received from him, particularly after he took to heavy drinking, increased when she began meeting her former lover in secret to resume their passionate love affair. Her tormented double life led Amy to seek a way out of it, firstly by freeing herself from her disastrous marriage. She acquired a quantity of arsenic and laced her husband's ale with it. He died the same day.

As soon as he was in his grave, Amy waved caution to the wind and blatantly began to court her lover, which caused the neighbours to gossip and suspect that something was wrong. Hutchinson's body was exhumed, and it was discovered that he had been poisoned by arsenic. Within a week of his death, Amy was arrested, charged with his murder, committed to Ely gaol, tried, found guilty and sentenced to death at the stake.

Stoically, she confessed her guilt, agreed that the sentence was just and prepared herself for her gruesome end. At the place of execution, she was tied to a stake. The executioner smeared tar on her face and hands and daubed pitch on her garments, then calmly stood by while a clergyman read a short formal prayer. The executioner then strangled her, kindled the fire, and left her to burn for an hour.

Some earlier methods of execution were equally barbaric. Henry VIII decreed that anyone found guilty of murder by poisoning their victim should be boiled to death. Margaret Day, a maidservant at a large house in King's Lynn, suffered this awful fate after poisoning her mistress and other members of the family. On the day of her execution, the terrified girl was forced to watch the fire being lit beneath a huge cauldron of water and wait until it reached boiling point. She was then lowered into the boiling water by gantry, raised and lowered time and time again until her anguished screams ceased and she was declared dead. Fortunately, this gruesome method of execution was seldom used, and was abolished when Henry's son, Edward VI, succeeded him as monarch.

Beheading was introduced by the Normans, but was almost exclusively used as a means of executing aristocrats and prominent members of the public who had broken the law and were sentenced to death. Hanging became the most common means of execution in Anglo Saxon times, and remained so in England until capital punishmemt was abolished in 1969.

Felons sentenced to death in bygone days had first to endure a most unpleasant stay in a county gaol. The majority of these were such loathsome places that those incarcerated in one were commonly said to be 'in durance vile'. A new inmate was obliged to pay what was termed 'garnish' to his fellow prisoners. At Cambridge, Ipswich and Norwich gaols the 'garnish' was set at one shilling, irrespective of the crime committed, except the crime of being in debt. Perversely, imprisoned debtors were obliged to pay double, or even treble 'garnish'.

Needless to say, many new inmates, especially debtors, were unable to meet the financial demands of the old lags, so were forced to give up most of their clothing in lieu of cash. The usual threat was: 'Pay or strip'. As if walking around in scant underclothes was not humiliating enough, the uncaring and mercenary gaoler added to a new inmate's misery by demanding charges for bedding, which was often nothing more than fresh straw, for loosening or removing leg irons and heavy chains, and for supplying extra food.

A prisoner's standard rations were usually only a twopenny loaf of bread per day, so if he had no relatives or friends to supplement his meagre sustenance, or was unable to pay the gaoler for extra food, he was so hungry when the small loaf was tossed to him at breakfast time that he usually scoffed the lot there and then, and starved for the rest of the day.

Many medieval castles, such as those at Cambridge, Colchester and Norwich, were adapted to serve as county gaols. The cells, which were generally underground, were cold, damp, windowless and lacked adequate sanitation. Such foul conditions made ideal breeding quarters for germs, as it was impossible to maintain cleanliness and hygiene. Diseases, such as smallpox, and a debilitating fever known as gaol distemper, regularly broke out, killing off far more prisoners than the executioner did in a year.

By the 18th century the old buildings used as gaols had become so dilapidated and neglected that the disgruntled inmates would scheme and sieze the slightest opportunity to escape, sometimes with success. Preventing escapes was of far more concern to the authorities than conditions inside the gaols, and priority was given to ensuring a getaway was almost impossible.

In Norwich Castle and Thetford Town gaol, prisoners were confined in deep, damp, underground dungeons which could be entered only by ladder. In Colchester Castle they were secured by heavy iron fetters to stakes hammered into the ground. But it was the Bishop of Ely, who then had jurisdiction of Ely gaol, who authorised the introduction of the most barbaric means of securing prisoners. Reluctant to spend money on making the old gaol more secure, he had prisoners chained down to iron bars fixed across the floor. A spiked metal collar clamped round the neck made it impossible for them to rest their heads on the ground, and an iron bar fixed across the legs prevented them changing position.

So many complaints and protests against this dreadful treatment were made that the bishop was obliged to discontinue it and grudgingly allocate money to repair the prison in 1764. Whatever work was carried out must have been limited to surface essentials however, because, by the 19th century, the gaol had again fallen into a sorry state owing to neglect. This, coupled with the abolishment of the extreme measures of containing prisoners, led to a considerable increase in the number of escapes.

Security became so lax that in November 1800, James Thompson, who had been imprisoned in Ely gaol awaiting trial for stealing a horse since 1798, simply walked out without being questioned. He was dressed in what was

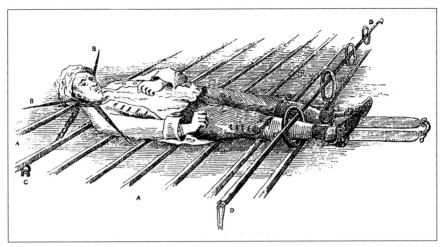

A prisoner chained to the floor in Ely goal.

described as a 'snuff coloured coat, a yellow-striped waistcoat, corduroy breeches, a pair of new shoes, and a very good hat' in a public notice that included the inducement of a ten guinea reward for information leading to Thompson's recapture. His taste of freedom did not last long and he was soon back in Ely gaol.

Extreme precautions must have been taken to ensure that he could not escape again, because it was said that he gradually 'went out of his mind'. But when he was eventually brought to trial in 1801, the court declared him to be 'no maniac', found him guilty, and sentenced him to death by hanging.

Precautions taken to keep Thompson in Ely gaol after his recapture proved ineffective regarding general security, because escapes from the place became even more common, as they did from most East Anglian prisons.

Mary Hudson, a thirty five year-old spinster, imprisoned in Norwich Castle in 1808 for various felonies, spent several nights chipping bricks from the wall of her cell, concealing them beneath her bed and loosely replacing them before daylight, until she had made an aperture large enough to make her escape. It was suspected that Thomas Cooke, a pedlar from Yarmouth, who frequently visted Mary, assisted her planned escape and that they had fled the district together, passing as husband and wife. But in spite of a ten guinea reward offered for information leading to their apprehension, neither was ever traced.

Daniel Dawson's plan to escape from Cambridge Castle in 1812 probably failed because of his own carelessness in giving instructions to his wife in writing, asking her to smuggle a small hacksaw into the prison and disclosing full details of his plan. Imprisoned for dosing racehorses with poison at Newmarket, Dawson pleaded that he had been the dupe of unscrupulous bookmakers and had only intended to give the horses enough poison to slow them down to prevent them from winning a race and not to kill or harm them. This made no impression on the judges, who sentenced him to death.

Desperate to prevent the hangman from ending his life, Dawson cast caution aside by handing the letter, diclosing his plan of escape, to his wife in the presence of gaoler Robert Orridge. The gaoler seized it and immediately had him secured by ball and chains. A scaffold was erected at the top of Cambridge Castle, specifically for Dawson's execution, on August 8, 1812, which was a market day. Some 12,000 spectators gathered and watched as he embraced his tearful wife in an emotional parting, and spent twenty minutes in prayer before being led to the gallows and publically dispatched.

Another Cambridge prison was the Bridewell, commonly known as the Spinning House. According to the historian Edmund Carter, writing in 1753, the place was used mainly for 'the confinement of lewd women'. Carter also remarked that the town crier frequently visited the prison 'to discipline the ladies of pleasure with his whip'.

Elizabeth Butchill, a bed-maker at Trinity College, who lived with her aunt and uncle, was highly regarded by her employers as a quiet, modest, hard-working young woman. She managed to conduct her many love affairs in secret until she became pregnant by one of the students. Somehow she succeeded in concealing the pregnancy, and gave birth to her unwanted child unaided on January 6, 1780.

Fearful that her aunt and uncle would hear the new-born baby's cries, she slapped its head time and again until she was satisfied it would never cry again. Then, mustering all her strength, she carried the tiny, lifeless body to the outside privy and shoved it down one of the holes that emptied directly into the river, where the dead body was discovered floating the following morning. Unfortunately for Elizabeth, her uncle happened to be passing her room at the time she was giving birth and, having heard the baby's cries, suspected that the child might be hers, and reported his suspicions to the authorities.

A surgeon was engaged to examine Elizabeth. She broke down during the examination, admitted that the child was hers and told how she had disposed of it. She was brought to trial, judged guilty of murder and, in spite of being ill and on the verge of insanity, was publically executed on March 17, 1780. Many of the thousands who attended wept in pity as she knelt in prayer and called upon Jesus Christ for mercy before she was led to the gallows.

Young Sarah Lloyd, a native of Naughton, Suffolk, took employment as a maidservant to a Mrs Syer, who lived in Hadleigh, and earned the complete trust of her mistress after serving her well for several months. Sarah's undoing was to fall in love with a rogue called Joseph Clarke, who persuaded her to leave the kitchen door open one night so that he could enter and steal whatever valuables he could find.

Sarah, besotted by his charms, complied with his request but, not content with robbery, Clarke set the house ablaze before leaving. Fortunately, the fire was soon exstinguished, but Sarah could not be found the following morning when investigations attributed the fire to arson. Many valuable items were missing, including a gold watch and ten gold guinea coins. Suspicion eventually fell on Sarah, who was soon tracked down and charged with burglary and arson, and imprisoned in Bury St Edmunds' gaol.

During her three months confinement awaiting trial, she repeatedly insisted that Joseph Clarke was the guilty party but evidence given against him at the trial was so flimsy that he was acquitted, whereas Sarah was pronounced guilty and sentenced to death by hanging. Wearing a white dress, trimmed with black ribbons, she was led to the scaffold on April 23, 1800. Several women in the large crowd that had gathered broke into hysterical sobbing when she spoke her last words: 'I hope I shall be an example to all', the meaning of which may not be clear in print after all this time, but they were obviously meant as a warning to other young girls about the disastrous consequences of falling for the charms of a scheming, lying rogue such as Clarke.

As soon as he was acquitted and released from prison, Clarke joined the army and, after training, was posted to the East Indies. In 1802 he caught a fever and became seriously ill. Before he died, he confessed that he had robbed and set fire to the house in Hadleigh, and that Sarah Lloyd was completely innocent. He had merely used her to gain access to the house.

Although burglary was a capital offence, it was one of the most common crimes, and more people were executed for burglary than for murder. The poor, driven by desperation to improve their miserable lot, and envious of the wealth of their employers, were constantly tempted to take a chance on resorting to robbery, even though they knew what the consequences would be if they were caught.

William Grimshaw, a Cambridge chimney sweep, tired of relying on infrequent calls for his services, took such a chance on the night of January 24, 1801, two months after he had last swept the chimneys of Alderman Joseph Butcher's house. Butcher had engaged Grimshaw a few times before, and the sweep was allowed entry to the house through the kitchen door. The display of silverware in the kitchen was so blatant that Grimshaw could not forget it, and weighed up how easy it would be to break into the kitchen.

On the January night he entered the kitchen, filled a sack with silverware, took it home, and hid it under the stairs, in the mistaken belief that suspicion would not fall on him. It did. His house was searched, the sack of stolen items was found, and he was arrested. At his trial, he was found guilty both on charges of burglary and of stealing property in excess of forty shillings in value, each offence carrying the death penalty, and he was hanged on March 28, 1801,

Although poaching was not a capital offence, seldom a day went by in rural areas without an illegally-had rabbit, hare or pheasant, stewing in the pot of a hungry family. Poaching became so common that an Act was passed in 1775 to the effect that any person found guilty of nocturnal poaching would be sentenced to six months in prison.

In spite of the harsher punishment, poaching increased as regular poachers, tempted by the profit they could make by selling their ill-gotten game to London market traders, formed themselves into organised gangs.

The land-owning gentry became so concerned about the game they were losing almost nightly, that they petitioned for poaching to be made a capital offence. Their petition resulted in a Act being passed in 1803 to the effect that an armed poacher, or one who resisted arrest, would be sentenced to death by hanging. A further Act was passed in 1816 which made unarmed poaching an offence liable to the punishment of transportation.

Neither of these Acts deterred the gangs from poaching. In fact they seemed to incite them into becoming even more daring, the thought of the profit they were making from successful raids overcoming any fear of the consequences if they were caught.

An armed gang, operating in the Sprowston area, near Norwich, raided the estate of Sir Edward Storey with the intention of bagging pheasants. The poachers managed to kill several brace before being intercepted by the game-keeper, March Buttifant, who, woken by gunfire, roused his assistant, William Everitt, and two other estate employees.

Satisfied with their spoils, the gang had no hesitation in dealing with anyone who attempted to prevent their getaway, and when challenged by Buttifant, two members of the gang, Miles Wiseman and Robert Whitaker, responded by firing their guns at him and his fellow gamekeepers, wounding Buttifant on his hand and lips, and Everitt in the shoulder.

In spite of their wounds, the gamekeepers fought back. Buttifant managed to fell Whitaker with the butt of his pistol and captured him. The rest of the gang fled. Whitaker was taken to the constable's house in Sprowston, where he disclosed the names of the rest of the gang. They were quickly rounded up, and joined him in gaol to await trial.

This took place at Thetford Assizes in 1824 and, although Miles Wiseman,

Robert Whitaker and two other members of the gang were found guilty of having shot at Buttifant and Everitt with intent to murder and sentenced to death, all but Wiseman were reprieved.

Wiseman met his end on the scaffold on April 10, 1824, probably because he was the unlucky one to be selected for execution as a warning to other poachers carrying arms. Ironically, a few days after his ignominious burial in Hardingham churchyard, his body was dug up by resurrectionists, most likely destined for dissection in one of the lecture rooms at Cambridge University. Surgeons had the right to claim the bodies of executed felons, and this was usually made clear to the condemned person after he had been sentenced.

Dissection was the ultimate end for John Rudderham's body in 1766. Rudderham, a notorious West Norfolk rogue, had a long record of robbery and various other crimes short of murder, until he added that capital offence to his list on the night of October 9, 1765, when he barbariously bludgeoned Leonard Wilson to death in King's Lynn.

The reason for the savage attack was not recorded by the newspapers at the time. Rudderham fled to Bury St Edmunds, which raised suspicions that he was the murderer, and two constables were sent to arrest him. Narrowly escaping capture he once again took flight, but following the offer of a £20 reward, he was arrested in Chelmsford and escorted back to King's Lynn.

The man was contradictorily nicknamed Honest John, and was said to be so 'depraved and ignorant' that he had no knowledge of 'anything to do with Christianity'. Whilst awaiting execution, after being tried and found guilty, he was visited by a priest who asked him if he had heard of Jesus Christ. Rudderham replied: 'I do rather think that I have heard something of such a gentleman, though I cannot now remember what it was'.

In modern times he would have no doubt been pronounced guilty but insane, but a person's mental condition, if he had committed a capital offence, was of little consequence in those days. John Rudderham was publicly hanged in Lynn market place on January 10, 1766. His lifeless body was left dangling for several hours before it was taken down and delivered to a surgery for dissection by Lynn doctors.

No matter who it was, or where it came from, a dead body was merely material for investigative surgeons to dissect or experiment with to further their medical knowledge. Mary Shelly's Frankenstein is perhaps tame stuff to what went on, and perhaps still does, behind closed laboratory doors in attempts to restore life to a dead body.

In August 1819, Professor Cumming eagerly awaited delivery of the body of twenty three year-old Thomas Weems, who had been executed at Cambridge for strangling his wife. The professor had a makeshift laboratory in the Botanical Gardens where a huge and powerful galvanic battery had been constructed to perform electrical experiments on a suitable body; the dead Weems was ideal.

Cumming had believed for some time that galvanism was the very spark of life, and could convert a lifeless body into a suspended state of animation. He attached wires to the nerves of various parts of Weems' body, making an electrical circuit, then began experimenting by charging the body with electricity. After an hour he gave up, disappointed that it produced nothing except contortions of the facial muscles, and the opening and closing of a fist with considerable force, but had no effect on the brain. Disillusioned, Professor Cumming consigned Weems' body to the surgeons for dissection and gave up attempting to restore life to the dead.

After Richard Nockolds had been hanged at Norwich on April 9, 1831, for setting fire to a farmer's hay stacks at Swanton Morley, his widow displayed his body in her little cottage in the nearby village of Pockthorpe, and raised a considerable sum of money from the curious and sympathetic public who came to view it.

The bodies of executed murderers were often tarred and left dangling in chains from a gibbet for years, at or near the place where the crime had been perpetrated, as a warning of the fate awaiting others who committed murder. The most famous gibbet in Suffolk was that erected on Blythburgh Common for suspending the body of Tobias Gill, an army drummer, whose regiment was encamped at Blythburgh.

Gill, a negro, commonly known as Black Toby, had already earned himself the reputation of being a drunken brawler and womaniser before he choked pretty Ann Blakemore to death when she fiercely resisted his attempt to rape her on Walberswick Common after a heavy drinking session at a nearby inn. When Ann's body was discovered the following morning, enquiries soon led to the arrest of Gill, who was taken to Bury St Edmunds' gaol, to await trial at the next Assize.

Found guilty, Gill was hanged on September 14, 1750. His body was then transported to Blythburgh and hung in chains from a gibbet near the spot where he had murdered Ann Blakemore. His grisly remains swung there for several years. The path across the common became known as Toby's Walk.

Travellers on the Great North Road in the late 18th century were reminded of the crime of Gervase Matcham for several years whenever they passed a gibbet erected near Alconbury, from which his corpse was suspended until it rotted away and fell apart, leaving only the skull.

Matcham, after serving in the navy, had enlisted in the 49th Foot Regiment of the army, which was stationed at Alconbury. Shortly after joining, he was entrusted to collect the soldiers' pay from the unit's headquarters at Doddington Hall, accompanied by a drummer boy named Benjamin Jones. The temptation to keep the money proved too much for Matcham. On the way back, he suddenly seized Benjamin, cut his throat and, satisfied that he was dead, threw his body into a ditch and fled north to Yorkshire with the cash.

Ironically, shortly after his arrival in that county, he was press-ganged into re-joining the navy, and completed his term of service without ever being suspected of deserting the army, or of committing murder.

Of course, when he failed to turn up with the payroll at Alconbury, an extensive search was made for him and the drummer boy, but several days passed before Benjamin's body was found in the ditch. All efforts to trace Matcham were unsuccessful at the time, and he may have remained free all his life if his conscience, or the affects of several pints of ale, had not got the better of him shortly after his discharge from the navy in 1786.

Journeying across Salisbury Plain, he stopped at an inn, but before he entered, he supposedly had a vision of Jesus Christ on one side of the road and the drummer boy on the other. The experience so unnerved him that, after brooding on it over his frequently replenished tankard, he confessed his crime to the astonished regulars, who called in the law officers. They arrested him on the spot and escorted him to Huntingdon for trial, at which he was found guilty and sentenced to death by hanging.

The corpses of murderers sentenced to hang were not always left to rot on wayside gibbets indefinitely. Home Secretary Robert Peel was so sickened by the sight of the rotting remains of murderer John Rolf, suspended from a 34ft high gibbet erected near Littleport, when he passed by on a visit to the Earl of Leicester's home in North Norfolk, that he ordered its removal.

Rolf, a vicious and unprincipled ruffian, had taken to earning a living by poaching in partnership with John Landen. While poaching on the night of January 29, 1823, Rolf suddenly turned on Landen, without apparent reason, bludgeoned him to death and robbed him of his silver watch, the few coins in his pockets, and even his boots, then buried him in a shallow grave.

Landen's body was discovered by a shooting party the next day. Rolf, wearing the dead man's boots, was immediately arrested and taken to Ely gaol, where he admitted his guilt. He was hanged at Ely on February 24, 1823. His body was then tarred and taken to Littleport and suspended from the gibbet that Robert Peel later ordered to be removed.

In spite of numerous types of crimes being punishable by death, there were only twenty one executions in Cambridge between 1780 and 1880, seven of which were for murder, the others for such crimes as rape, burglary, arson, and forgery.

A public execution was considered a rare spectacle, not to be missed, and usually attracted thousands. When Elizabeth Jefferies, who had been sentenced to death for the murder of her uncle in 1752, left Chelmsford gaol, fettered and chained in a cart, crowds lined the streets along the twenty mile route to Walthamstow where she was to be executed. Wooden stands had been erected at Walthamstow so that the morbid spectators would have a good view of the scaffold and Elizabeth's end.

A double execution at Norwich on August 24, 1822, was proceeded by a parade more befitting a civic celebration. Having been condemned to death for burglary, James Smith and Henry Carter, arms pinioned and necks bared, were seated on their own coffins in a cart covered with black cloth, and conveyed to a scaffold erected on the Castle Meadows from St Giles Street gaol, at the rear of a procession of dignatories.

The procession was headed by the under-sheriffs, followed by the sheriff and the chaplain of the gaol, all on horseback. Next came a Wesleyan minister in a mourning coach and, last of all, the cart carrying the condemned men. After the hanging, the bodies were laid in their coffins and ceremoniously carried to the house of Carter's parents by twelve bearers, where they were left on display before being buried in St Margaret's churchyard.

Several of the more squeamish in the vast crowd that gathered to watch the execution of Peter Donahue at King's Lynn on November 30, 1801, must have regretted doing so when the hanging went wrong. Donahue, a sergeant in the 30th Regiment of Foot, had been sentenced to death for forging a Bank of England note. Because of the clumsy fitting of the rope round his neck by the hangman, he was left writhing and struggling for several minutes after the drop, with blood gushing from his mouth and nose, as he slowly strangled.

Another gruesome execution was that of John Pycraft at Norwich on August 16, 1819. Pycraft, sentenced to death for poisoning his infant child, was a small, slightly crippled man, and the hangman underestimated the necessary distance of drop. Realizing his mistake as Pycraft strangled helplessly at the end of the rope, the hangman calmly affixed weights to Pycraft's legs until, after eight minutes, the condemned wretch choked to death.

Public executions certainly drew thousands of spectators and executioners were perversely recognised as celebrities.

William Calcraft, who served as public hangman from 1829 to 1874, longer that anyone else, was undoubtedly the most famous of them all. Born in Little Baddow, Essex, about 1800, Calcraft first followed his father's trade as a shoemaker in the village, but moved to London when he married and secured a job as a night watchman in a brewery.

In 1828 he was engaged as assistant hangman at a double execution in

William Calcraft, executioner, at work.

Lincoln, which led to his being employed at Newgate prison to flog juvenile offenders. A year later, Home Secretary, Sir Robert Peel, appointed him hangman at a weekly wage of one guinea, which he supplemented by continuing his shoemending business.

The majority of towns and cities did not employ a resident hangman, so Calcraft's services were in demand far and wide. A hard man, seemingly devoid of compassion, he would often swing on the legs of a choking and struggling wretch helplessly dangling from the ill-fitted noose, in an attempt to hasten his end.

Nevertheless, although he never mastered the art of his grisly trade, he was never short of unwilling customers. Journeying all over the country carrying out executions with thousands of people watching his every move, naturally made Calcraft an easily recognisable figure of morbid interest. Oddly enough, he was averse to being recognised on journeys, and often tried to disguise himself and disclaim his true identity if someone questioned him. After hanging Robert Brigstock at Ely in April 1834, for instance, he disguised himself as a farmer.

A public hanging in the small Fenland city was a rarity, and an immense crowd gathered to witness the execution of Brigstock, who had been sentenced to death for setting fire to the stable and chaff house of William Vawser in the town of March. Having performed his duty, Calcraft boarded the Lynn Rover coach hoping for a journey back to London free from attention. But Jack Goodwin, the coach guard, observing a length of rope in Calcraft's baggage, became suspicious and addressed him by name.

Calcraft said he was mistaken, but Goodwin replied: 'I am not. I saw you perform on three criminals at the Old Bailey,' and kept on at the hangman until he admitted his true identity. The two then engaged in amiable conversation, most of which was about Calcraft's experiences. When the coach arrived in London, Calcraft thanked Goodwin for a pleasant ride and assured him that if ever he had the pleasure of hanging him, he would make his end as comfortable as possible by soaping the rope.

Calcraft officiated at several public hangings in East Anglia during his long reign. The occasions always attracted thousands of people, who boosted local trade and, colourfully dressed, created a festival atmosphere. Vendors sold gallows literature in the streets, fiddlers played while vocalists sang songs about the crime, the criminal, the victim and, of course, the hangman.

Calcraft visited Norwich in 1867 to hang Hubbard Lingley, who had been sentenced to death for killing his uncle with a shotgun. By this time public hangings were causing so much disruption and controversy that Parliament was obliged to pass a Bill in 1868, stating that all executions must be conducted behind prison walls in private, which at least spared condemned criminals prolonged humiliation.

The executioner's clumsiness probably influenced the passing of the Bill, as the press always gave a detailed report of public hangings, which included the performance of the hangman. In an official report on capital punishment in 1864, it was stated that Calcraft's methods were 'very rough - as if he had been hanging a dog'. But a hangman's job was not easily filled, and Calcraft held it until he retired in 1874, when a man named Marwood succeeded him.

Marwood openly stated that he did not think much of Calcraft's methods and that his predecessor was lacking in skill because he came from a family of 'slow-worms', and choked his prisoners to death. But the public never had the opportunity to compare Marwood's methods with Calcraft's, because he and successive hangmen performed in the private confines of execution chambers.

A CORPSE FOR THE SURGEON

L ITTLE was known about the internal physical intricacies of the human body until the early 19th century. External operations, such as the amputation of limbs and removal of surface tumours, were usually carried out before that time by barber-surgeons, who probably gleaned their knowledge of anatomy from such written works as *De Humani Corpis Fabrica* (Vesalius 1543), or from dissecting pigs and other domesticated animals, which were easily obtainable at little or no cost.

Surgical operations of whatever nature were, of course, performed while the patient was fully conscious. It was not until after Sir Humphrey Davy, the eminent British scientist, and inventor of the miners' lamp, introduced nitrous oxide (laughing gas) as a means of anaesthetising patients undergoing dental surgery, that medical researchers gave serious thought to easing the traumas of those who had to face the surgeon's knife in abject terror and pain. However, there is no record of anyone bursting into uncontrollable laughter after having all his or her teeth extracted.

The main quest for centuries was the intricate study of the human body but, obviously, lifeless human bodies were not readily available for dissection, so something had to be done to obviate the shortage. Henry VIII was a firm supporter of medical research. In 1540 he chartered the Company of Barber-Surgeons, and granted it the right to claim the bodies of four executed felons a year on condition the corpses were collected from the gallows for dissection at lectures or demonstrations.

The Company of Barber-Surgeons was thus recognised as the principal medical body of the day, but not all the members were accustomed to giving a short back and sides in between performing operations. Barber-surgeon John Caius, who was born in Norwich in 1510, studied his craft in Italy under the famous anatomist Andreas Vesalius after completing his education at Gonville Hall, Cambridge. When he returned to England in 1544 he was appointed by Henry VIII as a lecturer in anatomy at the Barber-Surgeons Hall in London, and continued to lecture there and elsewhere for more than twenty years.

During this time he became personal physician to three successive sovereigns, namely Edward VI, Mary I and Elizabeth I, and was acknowledged as a pioneer of anatomy and as 'the most learned physician of the age'. Caius College, Cambridge, was named in his honour.

Queen Elizabeth I decreed that Caius was to receive an annual allocation of bodies of criminals or unknown strangers, whose deaths occurred in Cambridge, for dissection in his college laboratory.

Anatomy was not generally recognised as a subject taught at university until a professorship was established at Cambridge in 1707. On June 12 of that year, George Rolf was awarded the title of Professor of Anatomy, but had to wait another nine years before an official anatomical lecture room was set aside for him. The room was situated in a building at the corner of Silver Street and Queen's Lane, opposite Queen's College, and was perhaps then only given because it was deemed of no use to the University for any other purpose.

Unconcerned as to why he had been allocated the room, George Rolf set to work with renewed enthusiasm – until he ran out of bodies! Indeed, the shortage of bodies available for anatomical research was becoming such a problem that a clause was inserted in a Parliamentary Bill, that 'the bodies of persons executed for felony and other crimes should be given to the University of Cambridge for anatomical dissection', but it was subsequently withdrawn before the Bill was presented.

Rolf became increasingly frustrated by the shortage of bodies. So much so that he began to neglect his professional duties and, in spite of several warnings, was dismissed from his position and stripped of his title in 1728 for continual absence from office. His successor, Dr John Morgan, had no qualms about obtaining corpses from any source, and was quite willing to buy them from resurrectionists – an alternative name for bodysnatchers – whose profitable but illicit trade reached its peak in the mid-19th century because of the increasing demand for their grisly wares.

In the early days resurrectionists encountered little difficulty in stealing newly-buried bodies from churchyards in Cambridge and the surrounding villages in the small hours of the morning, and even gained unofficial support from the university students. For instance, in 1732 it was suspected that the missing body of a man interred in Ditton churchyard had been delivered to Emmanuel College for dissection by Dr Morgan, and a large concourse of townsfolk marched to the college armed with a warrant to search it. When they were refused admission they began tearing down a wall to gain entry, but the students united to defend the privacy of their territory. The disturbance reached such a peak that the town clerk was called to read the Riot Act, and the mob reluctantly dispersed.

Later, the constables searched the entire college, but found no body. It was discovered the following morning floating in the pond in the college close! No charges were pressed, but the disturbance and scandal necessitated the Senate, the university's governing authority, to pass a law forbidding the acceptance of corpses illegally acquired and supplied by resurrectionists – but the law had little or no effect.

In 1753, Charles Collignon was appointed Professor of Anatomy at Cambridge University. His emaciated appearance prompted the notable Cambridge historian, William Cole, to write: 'I consider him to be a most suitable person for the position, as he is a walking skeleton himself – nothing but skin and bone.' Collignon had no scruples when it came to secretly purchasing bodies from the resurrectionists. He carried on doing so with impunity for years, but had an unexpected shock when he was about to commence dissecting a corpse supplied by the London resurrectionists in 1768. Knife poised over the body, he calmly began his lecture to a class of eager students, then recoiled as he recognised the lifeless features of Lawrence Stern, a celebrated author of the day, who had been ceremonially buried in London just two days previously.

Making an excuse for suspending his demonstration, Collignon hastily arranged for Stern's corpse to be removed from the lecture room, but was unconcerned what happened to it as long as he could not be accused of illicitly receiving and dissecting the body of a well-known person. He was not to know that Stern's body would be kept at Cambridge University, and that many other lecturers would use the skeleton in the years to come to educate students of anatomy. Undeterred by the experience, Collignon continued to accept bodies from dubious sources until he retired.

His successor was the eccentric professor, Sir Busick Harwood, who became obsessed with dissecting bodies, no matter how they were obtained. He enjoyed his work so much that he would carve a joint of meat at Sunday dinner with the same meticulous ease and precision as he did a human body in the lecture room.

Although corpses were occasionally supplied to Cambridge University by resurrectionists from sources outside the region, the acquisition of bodies by the major London hospitals, most of which had established their own teaching laboratories, was mainly dependent on those supplied by the resurrectionists of East Anglia. Thus a lucrative trade sprang up between the resurrectionists and any surgeon, far and near, who was willing to pay the price for the delivery of a fresh corpse without question.

Newly-interred bodies were resurrected and regularly transported to London by stagecoach or carrier's wagon in trunks or boxes without the operator's knowlege of the grisly contents. But there were exceptions. On February 15,

1823, a large trunk wrapped in cloth was taken to the Norwich depot of the Telegraph stagecoach for despatch to London. As this was the fourth package of its kind delivered to the depot in as many days, an official became suspicious, detained the porter in charge and sent for a magistrate. When the trunk was opened it disclosed the body of an old man named Brundall, who had been buried in Lakenham churchyard two days earlier. The porter gave way under interrogation and confessed that he was acting under the instructions of a man named Collins.

Collins was duly arrested and committed to Norwich Castle gaol. The body of Brundall was replaced in its original coffin and re-buried in the grave from which it had been taken. There is little doubt that it was destined for the dissecting table of Astley Cooper (1768-1841), a native of Norfolk, whose brilliant career, after attending medical school, began as a lecturer in anatomy and surgery and culminated in the appointment of Professor of Anatomy to the Royal College of Surgeons and personal physician to the monarch. He was awarded a baronetcy for successfully removing a surface tumour from the head of King George IV.

Cooper's brilliance and his esteemed position probably protected him from the ignominy of arrest, which befell other surgeons who knowingly received and paid for corpses supplied by resurrectionists. He was even known to boast

Resurrectionists robbed 20 graves at St Nicholas, Great Yarmouth, in 1827.

that he could obtain the body of anyone deceased, irrespective of their station in life, and employed some of the most notorious gangs of resurrectionists of the time to keep him well supplied.

On rare occasions, when a lifeless human body was not available, Cooper would dissect whatever dead animal he could lay his hands on. Once he even dissected an elephant, which had died in the Tower of London menagerie, in the courtyard of St Thomas's Hospital. Cooper was at his happiest when he was up to his elbows in flesh and blood, and was undoubtedly one of the leading accomplices of the resurrectionists who got away with it. He openly stated his belief that: 'The law only enhances the price. It does not prevent exhumation!'

Nevertheless, relatives of the dead were becoming more concerned and distressed as burials became increasingly prone to desecration by resurrectionists. Late in 1827, George Beck, a baker living in Great Yarmouth, suspected that the grave of his recently buried wife, Elizabeth, in St Nicholas' churchyard, had been tampered with. Inspection confirmed his worst fears. The body had been removed from the coffin. The discovery caused others to examine the graves of their departed, and to everyone's horror it was found that more than twenty bodies had been taken. No effort was spared to catch the culprits, who proved to be William Barber and his son, Robert.

In a plea for leniency Robert turned King's Evidence, and described how he and his father had robbed the graves, packed the bodies in boxes and shipped them by wain to London, having been asked to do so by Thomas Vaughan, a professional resurrectionist, who was in the employ of none other than Astley Cooper.

When Vaughan was arrested and brought to Norwich to stand trial, Cooper paid his bail expenses and no doubt hoped for his acquittal so that he could resume supplying him with bodies from another area, but Vaughan was found guilty and was committed to the House of Correction for six months.

Although Cooper was perhaps as guilty as anyone for encouraging resurrectionists to ply their nefarious trade, he appears to have got away with it, even though he never denied collaborating, and rewarding those who served him. What happened to Vaughan when his sentence ended is not known, but Cooper made sure his wife did not suffer financial hardship during his internment. He gave her an initial payment of six pounds when her husband was sentenced, and ten shillings a week allowance while he was imprisoned.

The publicity surrounding the Vaughan case highlighted the enormity of the trade in dead human bodies, and people began taking precautions to protect the graves of their buried kin from desecration by bodysnatchers. A costly wrought iron coffin without screws or removeable parts, invented by Edward

Bridgman in 1818, was regarded as useless after bodysnatchers smashed one to pieces in 1823 and, uninterrupted, carried the corpse away.

In the cities, high iron railings and gates that could be locked at night were erected to enclose graveyards. Graves were dug deeper, and massive stones were placed over them. Those who could afford it contributed to the cost of building a watch-house and employed someone to keep an overnight watch therein for intruders.

Undeterred, the resurrectionists diverted their attention to the graveyards of isolated villages, where the populace could ill-afford such elaborate measures to protect their dead, although groups of armed volunteers were formed in some places to keep vigil around the churchyard in the chill night air. Some of these groups had minor successes, such as that at the churchyard in Bacton, Norfolk where, on a night in 1828, six men who had positioned themselves to keep watch over the grave of James Howlett, observed two men alight from a gig armed with spades at two o'clock in the morning.

The guards kept quiet and well-hidden until the intruders located the grave of Howlett and began digging. A guard immediately fired a gun and the bodysnatchers fled, one as best as he could hobble, because it was obvious that he had been hit in the leg. Although both men managed to get away in the darkness the watchers were well satisfied because they had saved the body of James Howlett from the dissecting table.

Resurrectionists who were occasionally interrupted and foiled in their attempts to steal bodies from other village graveyards, usually managed to escape to strike again elsewhere, spurred on by the profit they could make from supplying corpses to some of the most eminent surgeons in the land. Indeed, the demand for bodies became so great that gangs, whose sole and lucrative business was the supply of bodies to hungry laboratories, were formed.

When demand exceeds supply, corruption breeds more corruption, so it followed that bodysnatchers eventually resorted to murder, either directly or as accomplices to those who were even more mercenary, and evil enough to carry it out. Perhaps the most notorious pair of rogues who murdered purely for profit were William Burke and William Hare, who were brought to trial in 1829. Their gruesome activities can be read elsewhere.

Disclosures at the trial so horrified the public that medical practitioners began to seek an acceptable means of obtaining adequate supplies of bodies for dissection and research. At a meeting in January, 1829, the physician and surgeons of the Norfolk and Norwich Hospital concluded that 'if the practice of dissection in schools were to be neglected it would lead to the greatest aggravation of human misery as further knowledge could only be gained by mangling the living'. They did, however, agree that regulations for 'supplying the means for dissection' were necessary, and decided to petition Parliament for legislation based on their proposals – which were:

1) permitting bodies to be imported.

2) giving individuals the right to Will their own bodies for dissection.

3) transferrence of unknown and unclaimed bodies to public schools for dissection.

A Bill, which included the second and third proposal, was subsequently passed by Parliament, much to the disgruntlement of several surgeons, who continued to acquire corpses from whatever source and by whatever means they could.

The rebel surgeons therefore kept the bodysnatchers in business. A notorious partnership was formed by Charles Fowler, a chair-mender by trade, and an Irishman named Johnson Smith. These two concentrated on graveyards in the Ely area, but their run came to an end in December 1830 when they dug up the newly-buried body of Rebecca Shearman in St Mary's churchyard, Ely, packed it in a large hamper and took it to the wagon office of Marsh & Swan for conveyance to an address in London.

The office clerk became suspicious when he noticed an offensive smell coming from the hamper, and called the constables, who opened it to disclose its grisly contents. Fowler and Smith were identified as the culprits by the office clerk, and were arrested. They were brought to trial at the Isle of Ely Sessions in Wisbech on January 5, 1831, and were found guilty of desecrating the grave of Rebecca Shearman, and stealing her body. They were sentenced to twelve months' hard labour in the House of Correction at Wisbech – a relatively lenient sentence which did nothing to deter other bodysnatchers from continuing their profitable nocturnal activities for as long as there was a market for dead bodies.

Doctor William Clarke, Professor of Anatomy at Cambridge University, was always on the lookout for a suitable subject. Known affectionately as 'Bone Clarke' by his students, he almost caused a riot in the village of Barnwell in 1833 following his offer to pay all funeral expenses of a pauper named Porter, who died in his own dwelling, on condition that the body was transferred from Barnwell to the Anatomy School in Cambridge immediately after the funeral service.

Apparently Porter had no relatives living in the area and it fell upon the parish to bury him, so a few officials quietly accepted Clarke's offer to avoid a drain on parish funds. All went according to plan until Porter's body was privately transferred to the Anatomical School after the funeral service. The people of Barnwell demanded to know what had happened to it, and insisted

The Anatomical Museum, Cambridge, through the corner window of which bodies were passed for dissection in the lecture room.

on a public inquiry.

This was held in Trinity Parish Schoolroom, Cambridge, and was attended by more than 300 people, many of whom, unable to get in the overcrowded room, assembled outside. At the conclusion of the meeting, when a verdict was announced that the body had been illegally removed because the Act of Parliament stipulated that the transferrence of a body from one place to another was not legitimate unless approved by the majority of parish overseers, the crowd outside the schoolroom went wild.

Barnwell had six parish overseers but only three had signed the certificate of transfer. The crowd stoned the Anatomical School, broke the windows, smashed the doors, entered the building, and ransacked the place in search of Porter's body. The Mayor of Cambridge arrived, supported by several dignitaries from the university, and read the Riot Act, but retreated when his proclamation was greeted by a savage hail of stones. When the mob failed to locate Porter's body they eventually dispersed and thirty special constables were engaged to guard the building, but Dr Clarke gave up the body the next morning and it was conveyed to Barnwell in a hearse for burial.

The legitimate supply of corpses for anatomical research gradually became accepted by the public as an essential means of medical research into the cause and relief of human suffering, and many began stipulating in their Wills that their lifeless bodies was to be given up for dissection.

The gruesome business of bodysnatching thus came to an end, but there is no doubt that all who were directly or indirectly involved in the practice, either as profit-seeking resurrectionists, suppliers, carriers, willing receivers or enthusiastic dissectionists, helped to further anatomical knowledge and alleviate many physical ailments. Whether their consciences were ever stricken by the distress they caused is another matter.

KILL OR CURE

JOHN Addenbrooke, son of the vicar of West Bromwich, was accepted as a student at Catherine's Hall College, Cambridge, in 1697. At that time Cambridge University had become a mecca for students deciding to study medicine and anatomy. Such was John Addenbrooke's interest, but he first had to obtain an Arts degree.

After four years intensive study of the classics, astronomy, divinity and maths at Catherine Hall, he received his BA degree but continued studying the same subjects until he gained an MA in 1704. He then moved to Corpus Christi College to study medicine and was awarded his MD at the end of a six year course.

Little is known of his life in Cambridge thereafter, except that he set up his own medical practice in the town and was described by a contemporary as 'having many oddities'. One of these was said to be an interest in necromancy, in which black art he was reputed to be able to reveal things past, advise on the present and forecast future events by communicating with the devil. He even used his diabolical skills to forecast the day and hour of his own death.

Addenbrooke left Cambridge in 1712 and set up a practice in London, where he is said to have suffered bouts of mental disturbances. The condition probably made him decide to leave London and settle in Buntingford, where he died on January 7, 1719, within minutes of the time he had predicted he would die on that very day. He was only thirty nine years old, had contributed nothing towards the furtherance of medical science, and would have no doubt been forgotten had it not been for a section of his Will in which he bequeathed a substantial amount of money to be used for medical purposes – 'to hire, fit up, purchase or erect a building fit for a small physical hospital in the town of Cambridge for poor people, to be open to every sick person of that county, if room and revenue permitted.'

Addenbrooke stipulated that the Master and Fellows of Catherine Hall were to be appointed as trustees of the scheme but, owing to a lengthy wrangle with members of the Addenbrooke family, forty four years passed before alternative trustees were approved and appointed, and were able to buy a suitable plot of land in Trumpington Street, and commenced building a hospital.

The first Addenbrooke's Hospital.

It opened on October 13, 1766. Ann Perry, a Cambridge spinster, was appointed matron at a salary of £10 per annum, plus a gratuity of £5, to be given if she 'behaves well'. Miss Perry had no medical qualifications but seems to have obtained the position on the merits of her housekeeping skills. She had charge of the staff, consisting of two nurses, two kitchen servants and a porter, who were obliged to conform to the strict rules drawn up for the smooth running of the hospital. Although she remained a spinster, the staff had to address Anne Perry as Mrs, and Rule 98 stated that all nurses and servants must obey the matron as their mistress.

The matron's power over staff and patients was awesome and was reinforced by numerous other rules such as:

Rule 105. No male patients may go into the women's ward, and no women patients may go into the men's ward without leave from the matron.

Rule 106. Patients must not swear, curse, behave rudely or indecently, on pain of being discharged.

Rule 107. They must not presume to play cards, dice, or any other game, or to smoke anywhere within doors.

Rule 108. Patients who are able are to be employed in the service of the hospital in washing and ironing the linen, washing and cleaning the wards, and any other business the matron shall require of them.

Rule 109. Patients shall not presume to loiter about the hospital.

Although all the regulations and strict discipline make the place sound more like a prison, Addenbrooke's Hospital soon acquired a reputation for excellent residential care. During the first year of its active exsistence, only twenty six of the 263 patients who were admitted died.

Apart from the resident nurses, the medical staff consisted of three physicians and three surgeons, all of whom were connected with the university and ran their own private practices. They generally attended the hospital on Mondays, Wednesdays and Fridays.

There are no records of surgical operations performed, but it is known that one of the duties of the hospital porter was to attend every operation and hold the patient down or, if the operation took place at night, hold the candle. It is not clear if someone else was enlisted to hold the patient down while the porter was holding the candle during night operations, or whether he had to combine both tasks as best he could, but the success rate under difficult conditions must have been high, thanks to the skill of the surgeons.

They, and the physicians, were highly regarded. One of the physicians was Robert Glynn, who also had a private practice in Cambridge. An eccentric dresser, distinctive in his scarlet cloak and black tricorn hat, quick-tempered, argumentative and self-opinionated, he had little interest in the administration of the hospital, but was popular with patients, who travelled from all corners of East Anglia to consult him.

He is said to have made a fortune from his private practice, but never charged the clergy, Etonians or Cornishmen, and seems to have had an interest in herbal medicine, as he often prescribed a concoction called Huxham's Bark, usually to be taken with a glass of camomile tea. Dr Glynn seldom, if ever, resorted to blood-letting, which most of his contempories favoured when other treatments failed.

Blood-letting was widely practised by barber-surgeons who advertised and recommended it as a cure for most ills. In the early 18th century there were several women barber-surgeons in Norwich, many of whom had gained their knowledge from either watching or assisting their husbands. A widow named Hacon advertised that she 'cuts hair for either gentlemen or ladies to the greatest nicety' and 'also lets blood very finely, and to the poor for three-pence'. The widow of a certain Dr Taylor proclaimed that she could 'cure rheumatism, dropsy, scurvy, and many other diseases of the human body by bleeding with the blessing of God'.

At the same time, a woman named Mary Dimes, whose status and background is unknown, advertised that her Original Stone and Gravel Pills, which were made and sold exclusively by her, were acclaimed by both sexes as a cure for wind, colic, scurvy and rheumatism.

Undoubtedly, there was a difference of opinion between medical practitioners, irrespective of their qualifications, as to the the benefits of blood letting, but it was accepted as a common method of treatment for numerous ills until well into the next century. Dr Jonas Asplin, for one, was a fanatical believer in bleeding, and was known to express his disaproval if a patient he was called upon to visit had been under the care of someone else and had not been bled. He spent many years in France before returning home to Prittlewell in Essex, where he set up a practice in 1825. Entries in his diary probably portray why he had such a strong belief in the benefits of blood-letting.

On April 13, 1826, he recorded that he felt so ill that he was unable to visit a patient in Rochford and took to his bed. Two days later, a colleague, Mr Graham, called and bled him. On April 17 Dr Asplin wrote that he felt well enough to bleed himself of twenty two ounces of blood, after which he apparently recovered quickly and enjoyed good health for the next twelve months.

He was confined to bed again after falling from his horse while on his way to visit a patient in Shoebury on April 19, 1827. The driver of a carriage returning from market discovered him lying badly injured at the side of the road and conveyed him home, where he lay in agony for several days. Even so, he kept up his diary and, although no mention is made of who treated him, recorded on April 23, that 'after plentiful bleeding and leeching, I am this day enabled to turn myself in bed, but still have no power to move the right leg or thigh'. Some power must have returned by April 26 because he recorded that he was able to get up for the first time. He eventually made a full recovery.

Robert Glynn, the eccentric Cambridge physician, regularly journeyed across the Fens to Ely on horseback during his working life. Fenmen had great faith in his methods of treatment and probably gained some psychological benefit from his mustard plasters, which he invariably prescribed as a cure for the ague – a malaria type fever prevalent in the marshy fens. Dr Glynn no doubt knew the plasters served little purpose in reducing the fever, and he rarely charged the poor for them because he was aware and concerned that many fenmen were treating themselves with opium as a cure for not only ague, but for rheumatism and, increasingly, for various other ailments.

Opium was not new to the Fens. In fact fields of poppies had been widely grown for years for domestic purposes. When ready, the seeds of the poppies were infused in water to make what was called 'poppy tea', which was said to relieve pain. The poppy heads were then boiled with sugar and made into a syrup, to which a quantity of gin was added. This concoction was commonly taken as a tonic.

By the early 19th century opium prepared in alcohol was seen as a commercial proposition, and was sold in bottles as laudanum under various brand names, such as Godfrey's Cordial and Dutch Drops, by most chemists and grocers. It was also readily obtainable at Ely market, where it was said to be as common a sight on the stalls as cheese and butter. So blatant was the sale and use of the drug in Ely that the place was often referred to as the Opium-eating City.

Apart from medical purposes, laudanum was used by mothers to quieten troublesome babies and possibly even to get rid of illegitmate or unwanted children. In 1847 Sarah Scarborough of March was charged with murdering her son, William, by deliberately overdosing him with laudanum. The trial took place at Cambridge Spring Assizes in 1848 where it was established that Sarah was addicted to opium and regularly purchased two pennyworth of laudanum from Dawbarn's grocery shop. Witnesses swore that she was a kind, attentive mother, who always kept her child clean, well-fed and comfortably clothed. She was duly acquitted and William's death was attributed to an unfortunate accident.

Mary Rumbelow of Littleport was brought to trial at the same Assize court, charged with the manslaughter of her child by administering a fatal dose of laudanum. In her defence, Mary stated that she had purchased a pennyworth of laudanum from Cheesewright's grocery shop and had given the child a teaspoonful to help it sleep, but had been horrified to find it dead the next morning. Called to the stand, grocer Robert Cheesewright testified that he had obtained the laudanum from a reliable supplier in London, but now believed it to be of unusual strength. He explained that a pennyworth of laudanum equalled 160 drops and a teaspoonful about 60 drops, which was normally a safe dose. After summing up, the judge concluded that Mary Rumbelow meant her child no harm and directed an acquittal.

But in spite of the apparent danger and misuse of laudanum, no restrictions were placed on its sale – under various brand names – for many years. Opium was imported to keep pace with increasing demand, and poppy fields became rarer in the Fens. In 1867 the British Medical Association expressed concern about the vast quantity of opium being imported into the country, the bulk of which, it was said, was being procured for sale in the Fens. The association's report led to opium being added to the restricted list of the Pharmacy Act of 1868, but Fen folk were not easily denied their favoured remedy for ailments, and soon resumed growing poppies.

Rather than trust themselves or consult a qualified medical practitioner, many poor folk turned to a 'handyman' or 'handywoman' in times of illness. These were lay people who had no recognised medical experience but claimed to be able to treat patients for practically every known illness. There were many of them, and they probably acquired their name because at least one was near to hand in every town and village. Handymen invariably treated patients with herbal concoctions that had been passed down for generations, but many supplemented the medicines they prescribed with white magic rituals. One such handyman was James Murrell, who practised in Hadleigh, Essex. The seventh son of a seventh son, he was said to be more of a witch doctor than a medical man as he cast spells and exorcised his patients in attempts to cure them. He became known as The Cunning Man of Hadleigh but, in spite of such a questionable label, successfully ran his practice by treating animals as well as humans from 1812 until his death in 1860.

One of Murrell's contempories was Thomas Bedloe of Rawreth, Essex. He was known as the Cancer Quack because he claimed to be able to cure those afflicted by the disease. He, too, treated animals as well as humans, and displayed a sign outside his cottage which read: 'Thomas Bedloe, Hog, Dog and Cattle Doctor'.

Handymen and handywomen were mainly favoured by the poor, who could ill afford a qualified physician's fees, even though their unorthodox treatments were unproven and sometimes proved fatal. A typical case was that of Jane Bays of Cambridge, who consulted Kelly Booker, a part time handyman, but a gardener by trade. When Jane asked Booker if he could recommend something that would clear unsightly blemishes from her face, Booker gave her some powder and instructed her to take a quantity dissolved in water at intervals. Less than twenty four hours after taking the first dose Jane was dead.

Courts in those days seemed to have been more on the side of the handyman than his patient for, although Booker admitted that he had, through ignorance, prescribed a powerful corrosive sublimate, a poison, instead of purgative salts, the coroner recorded a verdict of death by misadventure and Booker continued prescribing.

Many amateur apothecaries manufactured their own medicines, which they advertised as cures for all types of diseases, whether the complaint was professionally recognised as curable or not. These amateur medics were seldom short of patients as the afflicted were only too anxious to try anything that held promise of easing their suffering. Sometimes their unorthordox cures worked, at least temporarily, and the delighted patient would give a glowing testament to the handyman.

In 1806, Henry Green, of King's Lynn, concocted a mixture which he called Green's Sudorific and Rheumatic Oil, and he claimed it could cure rheumatism, lumbago, sciatica and gout, and that he had already successfully treated a multiplicity of cases. His claim was backed by a testament from William Wilkinson of Lynn, who stated that he had been unable to work for many years because of severe rheumatism, but that after consuming a few bottles of

Green's Oil he was completely cured and had resumed his trade. Green sold his wonder mixture for five shillings a bottle and no doubt made a good profit from it. A Mr Gall, of Woodbridge, advertised his own Antibilious Pills in 1807 with a claim that they would bring speedy relief to sufferers of indigestion, flatulency, biliousness and headaches, and he added that they were particularly good 'for the effects of free living', whatever that meant.

Although travelling quacks were still to be seen occasionally, they were not as common a sight as they were in the 18th century when resident handymen were few and far between. Travelling quacks were skilled in the art of verbal persuasion, if nothing else, and claimed to be able to cure everything ranging from an irritating itch to terminal cancer. Most of them attributed their dubious talents to God, and mixed religion with their medicine, but they seldom stayed in the same place for long, probably to avoid complaints.

In November 1760 a quack calling himself Doctor Mylock Pheyaro announced that he had moved from Colchester to The Crown public house in Maldon, where he would continue to cure by the help of God a multitude of complaints, having since June of that year run successful clinics in Manningtree, Wyvenhoe, Saxmundham, Woodbridge and Hadleigh, where he claimed many people could testify to his abilities.

Another self-styled doctor, named Marks Leoni, rented a house in Great Yarmouth in 1788 and set up a clinic. He claimed to have studied medicine intensely in America for many years and had, 'by the blessing of God', discovered a remedy for most disorders, and was also able to restore sight to the blind. His claims were supported by a woman from Pakefield who made a public announcement that he had restored her sight.

Just how long Marks Leoni ran his clinic in Great Yarmouth is not known, but he no doubt moved on after a brief stay and could well have arrived in Norwich as 'Doctor Marks' some nine years later, boasting that he had practised medicine at the Clinik Hospital, Berlin, for ten years and had been personal physician to the King of Prussia.

Pseudo medical practitioners often used different names as they travelled from town to town, thus lessening the chances of their false credentials and dubious claims being questioned by the gullible public. A quack who called himself Doctor Nondmus duped many sick people in the Cambridge area in 1795 by claiming he was the resident apothecary at Addenbrooke's Hospital and had discovered cures for every known ailment. After making a fortune from his useless medicines he fled the area and was never seen again.

Certain quacks advocated what might today be called alternative medical treatment, although it is unlikely that 'Doctor' James Graham would now talk many people into joining his earth-bathing sessions, a communal treatment which he claimed would safely and speedily cure 'most of the diseases which medicine and surgery and all human means have failed to cure'. He assured female patients that although they would be required to lay naked under cover of earth, the treatment would in no way offend their delicacy or virtuousness, and he promised that full benefit would be felt after a few sessions.

Having enrolled many patients of both sexes, Graham had holes dug in the garden of a Mrs Darking, who lived opposite St John's Maddermarket, and he commenced his earth-bathing sessions – which consisted merely of the patient lying naked in the hole and being partly buried under loose earth for a time. The treatment earned Graham a fortune. There is no record of his methods ever being questioned and, like so many others of his kind, he eventually disappeared with his ill-gotten gains.

A Mr Carter of Potton, Bedfordshire, arrived in Littleport on July 31, 1805, with a claim that he could diagnose disease merely by examining people's urine, then prescibe an effective medicine to cure it. He gave notice that all persons consulting him should bring a measure of their early morning urine. Although Carter called himself a water-doctor, he became more commonly known as a 'piss-prophet'. He made no charge for examining the samples but made up for his free service on the sales of concoctions for treating whatever disease he supposedly diagnosed.

In September 1806 a notice was circulated in West Norfolk warning the public against consulting a travelling quack calling himself Doctor Fish, who was peddling his own concoction. Fish was apparently a sawyer by trade, but claimed to have developed the gift of being able to cure all diseases of the human body, and had conned several guineas out of many people in Mattishall and Dereham. The notice warned that Fish was last seen in the area of Downham Market, and it seems to have had the desired effect because he was never heard of again after it was circulated.

The death of a mother in labour, and her unborn child, frequently occurred when an incompetent handywoman mishandled the birth, and professionally trained midwives often found it necessary to verify their qualifications before fretful mothers-to-be would engage them. When Catherine Pearce moved from Colchester to Cambridge in 1814, she gave public notice that she had practised midwifery in Colchester for nine years, during which time she had attended upwards of 1,500 women in childbirth, all of whom had had a successful delivery, and that her sole reason for moving to Cambridge was so that she could be near close friends and relatives.

The earlier record of Elizabeth Cornish of Lowestoft, who died in 1775 at the age of eighty nine, and who delivered approximately 5,000 babies during her sixty years as a midwife, was broken by Phoebe Crewe, who practised as a midwife for forty years in Norwich until her death on May 28, 1817. She is said to have delivered 9,730 babies.

Although midwifery was, and still is, recognised as a female occupation, it was not unknown for a male to set himself up in the business. They were known as 'man-midwives', and one such was a young bachelor named Charles Haynes who founded his own midwifery practice in Norwich in 1729. He was seldom called upon to attend a woman in labour, and was eventually advised that if he wished to continue in business he should get married as it was not considered decent or proper for an unmarried man to tend a woman so intimately. Whether he ever married, either for love or in the hope of staying in business, is not known.

George Hatton of Royston advertised himself as 'Surgeon, apothecary and man-midwife' but boosted his uncertain income by giving inoculations. In 1773 he announced that for a guinea he would inoculate any person living within seven miles of Royston against smallpox. This was one of the few diseases that quacks claimed to cure. When news spread that it had hit a particular town, folk avoided the place, markets and fairs were cancelled, and trade slumped drastically until the all clear was given. Those who survived were invariably left with severe scarring, impaired sight or even blindness. The disease could spread rapidly, and was the most feared contagious illness.

Even so, when inoculation was first introduced into England from Turkey in 1721, it met with fierce opposition, mainly from church authorities, who condemned the practice as diabolical and heathenish, and warned that anyone associated with it would be sentenced to damnation. Whether the public took heed of the warning is neither here nor there, but few were bold enough to undergo a deep cut from a lancet and have a large amount of ripe matter from a smallpox postule inserted in it. This early method of inoculation against disease sometimes had the reverse effect, and the previously healthy patient became stricken with it.

Outbreaks of smallpox were almost uncontrollable in the 18th century. Between 1738 and 1744, one sixth of the inhabitants of Bury St Edmunds died from it, and the town was labelled 'the seat of death and terror'. When the disease reached Stowmarket in 1718 many of the poorest victims were taken to the sick-house where an allowance of wine, tobacco and strong beer was granted to the nurses to 'help them survive their arduous duties'.

The medical profession had tried for years to develop a safe and acceptable method of inoculation to combat the disease. Then, in 1761, Robert Sutton, a surgeon from Kenton, Suffolk, found that by making only a superficial cut in the skin and inserting a small amount of unripe matter from a smallpox postule, the patient suffered minimal discomfort in being immunised against smallpox. Sutton's son, Daniel, established a successful practice in Ingatestone, Essex, where he popularised his father's new method of inoculation. Other medical practitioners, near and far, quickly took up the method and the public flocked to their surgeries to be inoculated against the dreaded smallpox. In 1766, Daniel Sutton stated that he had inoculated 7,816 people against the disease, but was brought to trial at Chelmsford Assizes in July of that year, accused of causing an epidemic by encouraging infected persons into the town on market days for inoculation. The case was dismissed, as the charge was judged to have been made by persons having 'sinister and malicious prejudice'.

In 1772, a labourer from Waterbeach, who was anxious to have his two children inoculated, but could not afford the fee, managed to procure a small quantity of matter from a source in Cambridge. The following morning he spread the substance on slices of bread and butter and gave it to the hungry pair for breakfast. They eagerly consumed the revolting meal and soon developed mild symptoms of the disease, but rapidly recovered, unlike a good many folk who likewise could not afford the doctor's fee, and risked being inoculated by a handyman for a small charge.

Smallpox swept through the parish of Weston Longville, Norfolk, in 1791 not long after farrier John Reeve had inoculated several children against it. Reeve was more adept at pulling horses' teeth than giving inoculations to humans or treating them for medical afflictions. Nevertheless, before he dabbled disastrously with inoculations he had for many years been called upon by the villagers to relieve their dental problems, not always without complaint.

The vicar of Weston Longville, the Reverend James Woodforde, recorded in his diary on June 4, 1776 that, suffering from dreadful toothache, he called Reeve, who came and extracted the offending tooth 'shockingly bad', plus a piece of gum with it, causing him agonizing pain and a swollen face for a long time afterwards. The ordeal cost him two shillings and sixpence.

Mr Woodforde might have suffered less if he had made the short journey to Norwich, and been treated by one of the many itinerant dentists, some of whom were professionally skilled, who frequently visited the city. A married couple, Mr and Mrs Sedmon, arrived in Norwich in October 1790, took up rooms, and advertised a wide range of dental services, including cleaning, cure of toothache, extractions, treatment of gum diseases, and the fixing of artificial teeth.

False teeth at this time were more ornamental than practical, but Mr Sedmon claimed to be able to fit them firmly so that the wearer could eat and talk normally, and that they were indistinguishable from natural teeth. He charged ten shillings and sixpence for fitting one artificial tooth and twenty

The extraction of a tooth was always a painful ordeal.

guineas for a complete set. Sedmon's affluent patients sometimes asked him to fit natural teeth, which he supplied at two guineas per tooth, but they were either unaware or unconcerned that these had either been extracted from corpses in graveyards, from the dead lying on battlefields, or from poor people who were desperate enough to undergo the pain of having good teeth extracted for a small payment.

In 1797, an itinerant dentist named Z Florence offered the citizens of Norwich a top and toe service. He advertised himself as 'Dentist and Operator in Corns', and became well known for peddling what he called Powders of Rosina which, he guaranteed, would whiten and beautify the teeth, at four shillings a jar.

James Blair of Edinburgh was a reputable itinerant dentist who firmly believed that regular care of children's teeth would safeguard them from developing dental problems in later life. He rented rooms in Cambridge in December 1797 and stayed for three weeks, during which time he stressed the importance of children between the ages of six and fourteen looking after their teeth. No doubt he also recommended the daily use of his own patent mixture, Blair's Tooth Powder.

Perhaps the most unusual and noisy means of extracting a tooth was thought up by an eccentric doctor, by the name of Messenger Monsey. He would tie one end of a length of catgut round the tooth and the other end round a bullet, which he inserted in a pistol. When he pulled the trigger, the tooth would fly

71

out, assuming all went well. A native of Norwich, Monsey was often consulted by fellow native Sir Robert Walpole, the Prime Minister. It is said that Monsey shot out one of Walpole's teeth, in spite of the Prime Minister panicking before the end of the ordeal and shouting 'Stop! I've changed my mind!'

'But I haven't,' Monsey said, and pulled the trigger.

Bone-setting was another specialised medical service offered by amateurs as well as the professionally trained. John Minnett Mason, having learnt the art from his father, set up a bone-setting practice in Elm, Norfolk in 1826. His skill at manipulating joints to relieve pain, and treating fractures, soon earned him a reputation, and his services were in such demand that he made regular visits to King's Lynn and Holbeach. Having made a considerable fortune from the business, Mason bought a large house in Wisbech, where he settled down and became a much-respected citizen. In 1876 he was elected mayor.

Benjamin Gooch, a surgeon-apothecary who lived in Shotesham, Norfolk, was particularly interested in bone-setting. In 1758 he devised a wooden frame which held a broken limb straight until the fractured bone had knitted. The frame became known as Gooch's Splint and was widely used until it was replaced by plaster of paris. Gooch was one of the founders of the Norwich and Norfolk Hospital, which opened in 1771, and was appointed a senior consultant surgeon.

One of the most common operations performed in the hospital was the removal of stones from the bladder. The reason why so many poor people in Norfolk developed stones in the bladder has never been satisfactorily explained, but was thought to be a result of them seldom eating anything other than cereals. William Donne, a surgeon at the hospital from 1772 until 1800, performed 172 operations to remove stones during his stay, 147 of which were successful. Of the others, one patient gained some relief, and twenty four died either during the operation or because of complications that set in afterwards. Considering that a patient undergoing an operation for any complaint was given only a few drops of wine and words of assurance by way of an anaesthetic before he faced the surgeon's knife, Donne's record was remarkable, for major operations were not only dangerous, but the patient was all too aware of what was going on throughout, and suffered agonising pain.

Sir Humphrey Davy, the eminent British chemist, discovered the anaesthetic properties of nitrous oxide (laughing gas) as early as 1800, but it was not used until 1844, and then only by dentists in America, who declared it unsafe after experimenting on patients, unless it was mixed with oxygen.

Although ether was discovered in 1681, it was not recognised as a general anaesthetic until 1846, when American surgeons announced that a patient could be safely rendered unconscious for the duration of an operation and be oblivious of pain, simply by controlled inhalation of ether. The news quickly spread to Europe, and patients became less fearful of undergoing an operation on the assurance that they would be anaethetized by ether. It was first used in East Anglia at Addenbrooke's Hospital in January 1847 on a patient, who, after having a finger amputated, declared he had felt no pain or discomfort.

The lengthy era of agonizing surgery was over.

UNUSUAL CAUSES OF DEATH

W HEN Elizabeth Woodcock set off for Cambridge on her trusty steed, Tinker, from her home in Impington on the morning of February 2, 1799, the weather was reasonably bright and the roads clear. But by the time she had finished walking round the market purchasing provisions, the sky had darkened and the first flurries of snow began to fall and settle.

Undeterred by the threat of a heavy snowstorm, Elizabeth, a known tippler, could not resist stopping for a glass or two of gin at an inn in Bridge Street. When she left the inn the snow was falling heavily but, having activated her taste-buds, she was unable to pass the White Horse Inn without calling in for another drink. Although the storm had intensified and conditions underfoot were becoming treacherous when she left the White Horse, the thought of having another drink in the warm and friendly atmosphere of the Three Tuns spurred her on.

Elizabeth Woodcock suffering from the effects of her icy ordeal.

When, finally, she left Cambridge the storm was at its height. Tinker, his tipsy mistress clinging to his back, plodded along unrecognisable roads towards home, and continued to do so when Elizabeth fell off. Although she was only about a mile from her house, she had no idea of her whereabouts and, confused by drink and exhausted, she sheltered from the raging blizzard in the hollow of a hedge and fell asleep.

When she awoke, the drifting snow had completely covered the hollow and she remained trapped in her snow cave for four days, her only sustenance being some walnuts she found in a pocket of her cloak. She had no idea of the passage of time or whether it was day or night, but eventually thought of a way that might draw someone's attention to where she was imprisoned.

Mustering all her strength, she broke off a long twig from the hedge, tied a piece of red flannel to it and managed to push her improvised flag through the snow wall of the cave. It was not long before William Muncey, a member of the search party that had been looking for her, spotted the fluttering red flannel, and the party set to work digging her out of her icy prison. Suffering terribly from frostbite, she was transported home in a chaise, but soon lost all her fingers and toes. The only opiate she would take to relieve the pain was gin. She lingered until July 11, when death released her from further misery.

A rider was added to the entry of her death in the Impington parish register, which, whether actually true or not, was perhaps rather unkind considering the horrendous ordeal she had been through. It read: 'She was in a state of intoxication when she was lost. Her death was accelerated by spiritous liquors afterwards taken.'

An unexpected heavy snowstorm in February 1890 led to the death of the Reverend Ambrose Johnson, rector of Toftrees. After journeying to Norwich and consulting a solicitor about bankruptcy proceedings, he began walking to Thorpe Station, but took shelter beneath the shrubbery in Bramerton Hall gardens when a light snowstorm turned into a raging blizzard. The blizzard continued for hours and, numbed by the cold, the rector remained in his icy shelter for several days until he was discovered by a search party.

He was taken to the Norfolk and Norwich Hospital in a state of delirium, suffering from exposure and frostbite. One of his feet was so badly attacked by frostbite that it fell off before the surgeons could amputate it, as they did the other foot. Mentally deranged, he suffered agonising physical pain until he died on May 2, 1890.

Although severe winter frosts, leading to the freezing of dykes, drains and meres, were welcomed by ice skaters in the fens of Cambridgeshire, tragedies sometimes occurred which marred the pleasure of those participating in the seasonal sport. In January 1850, a young man named Harper was skating at speed along a frozen canal in the parish of Emneth when the ice suddenly gave way beneath him. He plunged into the merciless cold water and called for assistance, but the crowd standing on the bank of the canal had no idea how to rescue him. His lifeless body was eventually lifted from the canal by a manure drag.

Cold weather conditions were often recorded as the cause of death in coroner's reports, a percentage of which intimated that distress and death could have been avoided if the deceased had not been intoxicated.

In the early 19th century, Barnwell was noted for the number of prostitutes catering for the sexual pleasure of the undergraduates at Cambridge University. On the night of February 5, 1818, Lawrence Dundas, an undergraduate of Trinity College, having spent the evening drinking heavily with fellow students, set off on foot for Barnwell with the intent of engaging a prosititute to gratify his desires. He was quite drunk and had not gone far before he fell into a ditch, and his efforts to get out of the muddy water were in vain. Each time he reached the edge of the bank he slithered back in until, exhausted and overcome by the amount of alcohol he had consumed, he passed out. Dundas was discovered the next morning sitting in about eighteen inches of water, frozen to death. The coroner attributed his death to intoxication and prolonged exposure in severe weather conditions.

Some years earlier, on August 11, 1809, a heavy drinking session was primarily responsible for the death of wherryman Joseph Bexfield of Thurlton. After imbibing at the White Horse Inn at Thurlton Straithe, he suddenly remembered that he had left a parcel for his wife on the wherry, which was moored on the far side of treacherous marshes, and decided to collect it before he went home. Drink had given him false confidence and, ignoring the warnings of his fellow wherrymen that he should not attempt to cross the marsh at night, he set off determinedly. His bloated body was washed up on the bank of the River Yare, not far from Breydon Water, several days later.

The desire for a cup of tea led to the death of Sarah Brown, a widow who lived near Soham. On a day in October 1855 she went to fill a kettle from a drain opposite her cottage, as was her custom. It had been raining heavily and the sides of the drain were very slippery. Although Mrs Brown was used to collecting water from the drain in all weather conditions, she must have lost her footing, for she was found drowned in the drain shortly afterwards.

Drowning was a common cause of death in those days, for few people bothered to learn how to swim, or even how to hold their heads above water. William Crabb of Littleport drowned in the well of his back garden when his wife asked him to draw a bucket of water. It was said that he leaned over too far when he was hauling up the bucket and fell into the well. Hearing his cries for help, Mrs Crabb screamed for neighbours to assist her in getting him out but, by the time they did, he had drowned. Mrs Crabb and other members of the family could not believe William had fallen into the well by accident and were convinced that he had been pushed by someone who had a grudge against him, but this was never proven. He was buried in Littleport churchyard on March 11, 1850.

Before the various Factory Acts were passed in the mid and late 19th century, employers had no obligation to safeguard their employees against injury or death, and many workers toiled in dangerous conditions at their own risk. Injuries and deaths frequently occurred because of the lack of safety measures, but the worker, or his grieving dependents, had no claim against his employer for failing to ensure his safety.

In May 1877, David Shadbolt, a brickmaker employed at Swavesey brick factory, was engaged in tending a large clay-mixing tub, in which was a spindle with knives attached to pulverize the clay. The spindle was turned by a crossbeam pulled by a horse plodding round the tub. Noticing a piece of grass in the mix, Shadbolt leaned over the tub to remove it, but was struck on the head by the turning crossbeam and fell into the tub. The sharp blades of the spindle pulverised both the clay and poor Shadbolt into a gruesome mix as the horse continued its monotonous route round the tub.

Without some means of safeguard against people falling into large open containers of liquid, it was almost inevitable that sooner or later someone would do just that. Thomas Foyson, for instance, ran a small family business in Calver Street, Norwich, brewing vinegar. One day in February 1832, whilst leaning over a vat of vinegar to gauge the reading of the liquid – a routine procedure he had completed hundreds of times before – he slipped, fell into the vat, and drowned before anyone could get him out. His death was recorded as accidental and, although his widow and nine children were left to struggle on running the business, a Norwich newspaper reporting the tragedy stated that 'it is some consolation to add that his life was insured for a large sum'.

Drowning in beer might sound preferable to drowning in vinegar, but when it comes to gasping for life, it is of no consequence to a helpless victim what kind of liquid he is floundering in. Brothers Walter and John Morgan, from London, purchased a brewery in King Street, Norwich, in 1845. The brewery owned and supplied fifty four public houses in the Norwich area, and was busily engaged in meeting their demands. In May 1845, Walter was looking into one of the large brewing vats of brown ale when he lost his balance, fell in, and was drowned. At the inquest, medical experts stated that he had fallen into the vat because of dizziness, caused by inhaling fumes of carbonic acid gas arising from the fermenting beer.

The majority of employed workers accepted their lot of working in hazardous conditions without complaint, particularly those who were engaged in digging clunch from the pits at Cherry Hinton. They had to dig deep to extract the clunch, a substance used in the manufacture of bricks, and the deeper they dug, the greater the risk of a cave-in.

These were frequent, and sometimes resulted in fatalities. In September 1850, Samuel Flack and another man were busily engaged in extracting clunch from one of the deep pits owned by a Mr Emson when one side of the pit suddenly gave way and overwhelmed them. The incident was observed by nearby workers who hastened to their aid. They managed to locate and rescue Flack's companion unharmed, apart from bruises, but it took them half an hour to find Samuel's crushed and lifeless body and dig it out.

Accidents on the roads were common long before motorised transport monopolised them. Local newspapers regularly printed lengthy columns of incidents involving carts, wagons and stagecoaches. Farmer John Middleton, of Fen Drayton, set off for Baldock market with a cartload of cheese on October 8, 1829. Foolishly he stood on the shafts of the cart to give directions to a servant who was leading the horse on foot. When the cart began to gather speed down a hill near Creamer's Hatch, Middleton lost his balance and fell from the shafts beneath the wheels of the heavily-laden cart. Hearing his master's screams as the wheels passed over his loins, the servant managed to halt the cart and ran to the nearest house for assistance. But Middleton died in agony about half an hour later.

Icy conditions obviously brought more hazards to waggoners and coachmen, but most of them carried on working, regardless of the dangers. William Symonds, a waggoner of Cottenham, managed to get to Waterbeach Station in January 1854 to collect a ton and a half consignment of salt, but he found it difficult to lead the horse along the icy road with a heavily-laden wagon in tow. Although he clung firmly to the traces, he slipped on the ice and lost his hold on the traces just as he was nearing Landbeach. He shouted in vain at the horse to stop, then fell and a wheel of the wagon crushed his head, killing him.

Ice was also blamed for the death of stagecoach driver William Salter, who was crushed to death beneath his stagecoach when the horses slipped and the coach toppled over near Haddiscoe on the Yarmouth-Beccles road in October 1776. He was buried in Haddiscoe churchyard only yards away from the road where the accident occurred. The inscription on his tombstone reads:

> *His uphill work is chiefly done,*
> *His stage is ended, his race is run;*
> *One journey is remaining still,*
> *To climb up Sions holy hill,*
> *And now his faults are all forgiven,*
> *Elijah like drives up to heaven.*
> *Take the reward for all his pains,*
> *And leave to other hands the reins.*

The chances of a waggoner being killed by a public house sign falling on his head just as he was passing beneath it must be millions to one, but such an ending came to James Blood when he was returning to Royston from London in September 1733. The swinging sign of the George Inn in Royston High Street was a familiar sight, but its rusted hinges gave way at the very moment James passed beneath it on his way home, and it fell on to his head, killing him instantly.

Even though traffic was minimal before mechanised transport began to monopolize the roads, pedestrians, wending their way along what seemed to be a deserted route, could sometimes be taken unawares by a fast-approaching horse-drawn vehicle, and met their end if they failed to get out of its way in time. Eighty-year old John Fox was walking along a quiet road near Colney in December 1806 when he saw a wagon rapidly approaching. He tried to step aside to let it pass, but was too slow and was trampled to death by the horses. The following plea to drivers was inscribed on his tombstone:

Reader:
If thou drivest a team be careful
and endanger not the life of
another or thy own.

The perils of travelling by stagecoach have already been looked at, but sometimes accidents that befell passengers were due to their own negligence. Such was the case of the Reverend Gawain Braithwaite, a Fellow of St John's College, Cambridge, who, when returning to Cambridge on the Ipswich coach, either failed to hear or ignored the coachman's warning to passengers on the top of the coach to duck as it entered the yard of the Blue Boar Inn beneath a low archway. He was killed instantly when his head struck the archway. At the inquest the driver was acquitted of blame, several passengers testifying that he had given due warning.

By the mid 19th century, the era of stagecoach travel was nearing its end as the network of railways spread. Thousands of men were employed on laying tracks to link one town to another, and to build stations. In the agricultural areas of East Anglia, many farm labourers gave up working on the land, mainly because they could earn higher wages helping to construct the railway.

Thomas Rudderham of Hockwold, Norfolk, with a wife and two children to support, was one who quit farm labouring and found employment with the railway company, hoping to improve the lifestyle of his family; but the change only led to his death. The railway line from Ely to Brandon was nearing completion in 1847, when Thomas and a fellow worker named Charles Talbot, were engaged in applying gravel ballast to the track from wagons pulled by an engine travelling at about nine miles an hour.

When the train had covered about six miles, an axle-tree on the wagon next to the engine snapped, causing the second wagon to jump the rails. Although the third and fourth wagons remained on the line, the fifth, carrying Thomas

79

and Charles, overturned, throwing both men beneath the wheels of the sixth wagon. Charles Talbot was instantly crushed to death but Thomas Rudderham, suffering from horrible injuries, lingered in agony for a short while until death mercifully claimed him.

Since the time of their inauguration, railways have always been subject to accidents, and have ended the lives of many people, the majority of whom have been responsible for their own deaths due either to negligence, or to deliberately wishing to kill themselves.

When 74 year-old William Hood was returning to his home in Haslingfield from Cambridge one September night in 1886, he decided to take the shortest route by crossing the railway line at a place called Cantilope. He must have been either deaf or preoccupied because the noise of an approaching train failed to deter him and he was mangled to death. William Hood's tragic ending induced the railway authorities to instal notice boards, warning people to beware of approaching trains.

The 'flaming heart' gravestone in Burwell churchyard.
Courtesy of The
Cambridgeshire Collection.

Fire precautions at public gatherings were unheard of in 1727 when a company of puppeteers on their way to Stourbridge Fair, Cambridge, stopped at Burwell and hired a barn to present a one-night show to the villagers. Entertainment was a rarity in the small village, and so many people flocked to the barn that the doors had to be closed and locked when it was filled to capacity. Not long after the show had commenced, the barn began to fill with smoke, and the audience panicked when they realized that some of the bales of straw that had been brought in for them to sit on were on fire. They rushed to get out of the barn as the flames spread, but the closed and barred doors prevented them escaping from what rapidly became an inferno.

The people outside, hearing the screams of those inside, tried vainly to force open the doors until the roof of the barn collapsed, followed by an ominous silence. The next morning, the unrecognisable remains of seventy six people were recovered from the barn and were buried in two communal graves in the churchyard. Two years later, the Reverend Thomas Giddons, recording the tragedy, insensitively wrote 'that if the persons that perished had not been sinners, they would not have been sufferers'.

Richard Whitaker of Hadstock was blamed for starting the fire by placing a

The collapse of the suspension bridge at Great Yarmouth, when 130 drowned.

lighted lantern too close to the bales of straw. He was brought to trial at Cambridge March Assizes and strongly protested that he was innocent. Although he was acquitted owing to lack of proof, there is little doubt that seventy six people were burnt to death because of the unfortunate man's carelessness, and the incident must have haunted him for the rest of his life.

Death by drowning befell nine year-old Joseph Livingstone and his six year-old sister Matilda, as well as many others, on May 2,1845, when Wlliam Cooke's Circus visited Great Yarmouth. To attract the public to the show it was announced that Nelson the clown would sail down the River Bure in a common washtub towed by four geese. The best vantage point to view the unusual spectacle was a suspension bridge over the river. The bridge quickly became crowded.

When Nelson and the feathered team pulling his strange craft came into view, the crowd on the bridge rushed to the side he was approaching. The uneven weight caused the frail bridge to collapse, and everyone on it, the majority of whom were children, plunged into the river. Every available boat moored nearby set out to rescue them, as few of the gasping victims could swim, but although several were saved from a watery death, 130 people perished in the River Bure on that day, including James and Matilda Livingstone who had looked forward to an exciting trip to the circus.

MEN OF THE CLOTH

IN OLDEN times, the parish priest, whether titled Rector or Vicar, was commonly referred to as the parson. If he were unpopular, he would also be called many other uncomplimentary names best left to the imagination.

The parish priest was a leading and powerful figure in the community. Apart from attending to church affairs, he was usually appointed chairman of the Vestry. This was the forerunner of the parish council, and the committee was empowered to levy rates for poor relief, appoint the parish constable and other parish officials, allocate whatever amount it decided was needed for the maintainance of the highways, and deal with all community matters.

Land owned by the church, known as glebe land, was allocated to the parson to maintain and farm. If he were not familiar with farming, he would let the land to a tenant.

John Crackenthorpe, rector of Fowlmere, Cambridgeshire (1666-1719), employed several men to farm his extensive glebe land. The majority of his regular workmen lived in rented cottages on the farm. Although charging them rent, the rector's meticulously kept accounts show that he did not pay his workmen a standard weekly wage but paid them by the job.

John Watson, one of the tenants, and probably a thatcher by trade, was paid 8s 3d after spending five and a half days thatching the Parsonage barn. For another half day's work repairing the thatch on the new barn, he was paid 9d. But when a severe storm blew some of the thatch off the new barn several days later, Crackenthorpe expected Watson to repair the damage for nothing.

The rector seems to have devoted more time to looking after his own financial interests than he did tending to the spiritual needs of his flock. Several of his workmen had their own smallholdings and were allowed to keep their cattle in his paddock during the winter months for a nominal amount. They were also obliged to pay him tithes (the tithe was a tax levied on farmers to support the clergy and the church, and was supposed to be one tenth of the produce but was commonly paid in a set cash amount).

The Reverend James Woodford, vicar of Weston Longville, Norfolk (1774-1803), was just the opposite to John Crackenthorpe when it came to looking after the welfare of his parishioners. Every year he held a 'Tithe Frolic' for the farmers in the parish in December and bore all the expenses himself. After paying their tithes, the farmers were welcomed to the Parsonage House, where an abundant array of food and drink awaited them, including sirloin of roast beef, leg of mutton, rabbit, salted fish, and plenty of plum pudding. Drink flowed freely. Gallons of punch, wine, rum and strong beer – the farmers' favourite tipple – were consumed, and the majority of those attending must have returned home drunk.

The beer was invariably home-brewed at the parsonage, and was certainly strong. On one occasion, after the sludge from an exhausted barrel had been tipped and left in the yard, two of the parson's pigs located it and scoffed the lot. They remained drunk for two days, and no-one could do anything with them until they had sobered.

Few other parsons were as generous, or as understanding about tithe collections and the welfare of parishioners. John Vachell, for instance, vicar of Littleport, Cambridgeshire (1795-1830), gave priority to his duties as a magistrate. He had no qualms about bringing a parishioner to court, particularly if it were for non-payment of tithes. When Henry Martin, a prominent and wealthy farmer in the parish, delayed paying tithes on thirty seven acres of land set aside for growing oats, Vachell showed no favour by taking Martin to court to legally secure his dues.

Several other parishioners fell foul of Vachell and were treated severely when they were summoned to appear before him in court. He became extremely unpopular in the parish, and attendance at St George's church rapidly decreased – to the extent that it was reported that the congregation was very small, often consisting of just a few rude and uneducated children.

Times were very hard, particularly for the agricultural workers during the depression that followed the end of the Napoleonic Wars. Men were either thrown out of work and forced to rely on the generosity of the Overseers for Poor Relief from parish funds, or struggled to exist on low wages. To his credit, Vachell occasionally boiled a sheep to help relieve the hunger of the poor, but discontent was rife, and tension in the community increased until it reached the point of explosion.

One can read the full story of the Littleport and Ely Riots of 1816 elsewhere. Enough to say here that the angry workers, and their supporters, held a meeting and decided to take action against those in the locality whom they believed were responsible for their plight. The Reverend Vachell was one of their primary targets. He had retired for the night when he was disturbed by the raucous shouts of the mob as they approached the vicarage. Sensing the reason, he armed himself with a pistol, opened the front door and threatened to shoot anyone who entered, then read the Riot Act, which made no impression on the rioters. Three of them overpowered and disarmed him and, fearing for the safety of his wife and children, he called them to flee from the vicarage with him. The family ran part way to Ely in their night attire before they were picked up by a farmer driving a gig. The first thing Vachell did when they arrived in Ely was report the disturbance to the city magistrates.

In the meantime, the rioters ransacked the vicarage, breaking every window, wrecked the greenhouse, smashed all the kitchen crockery on the gravestones in the churchyard, and left little undamaged. They went on to ransack shops and houses in the town, and then marched to Ely to gain support.

Having been forwarned by Vachell, the city magistrates had sent for military assistance from garrisons at Cambridge and Bury St Edmunds, and detachments of troops were deployed to Littleport and Ely. The Reverend Sir Henry Bate Dudley, vicar of Willingham, and a magistrate, was put in charge of all who were engaged in suppressing the riot.

Bate Dudley was a force to be reckoned with himself. Known as 'the fighting parson' after earlier incidents in which anyone who upset him, and accepted his challenge of physical combat, regretted doing so. It is said that he spread fear amongst the rioters during their last stand at Littleport, in spite of receiving a blow on the head from one of the more daring. Undoubtedly he played a leading part in quelling the riot and rounding up the participants, and would perhaps have been better suited to a military career than that of a clergyman, for it was generally reported that he was good with fists, pistols and sword, but his sermons were of 'inferior quality'. Even so, he became a canon of Ely Cathedral in 1817.

The Reverend Vachell never returned to Littleport and lived in seclusion with his family at Aldburgh, on the Suffolk coast, until his death in 1830.

Another parson who enjoyed playing the part of a military man was Thomas Shield, vicar of Royston. He was in his element during the Napoleonic Wars, when England was under constant threat of invasion. As captain of a body of men who formed themselves into a brigade known as the Royston and Barkway Volunteer Infantry Corps, he would don his uniform on Sunday mornings, cover it with his surplice and then, after giving a long, patriotic sermon at the church, slip off the surplice and hasten to march his troops through the town. The corps band, led by the parish clerk, fronted the parade. Sheild would call a halt when the parade reached Royston Heath, bring his troops into line for inspection, then drill them for the rest of the afternoon.

Clergymen were generally easily recognised by their standard dress of black knee breeches, black buckled shoes, a black cocked hat and black cassock, a powdered wig being the only contrast to their funereal attire.

Certain eccentric parsons, however, were equally recognisable by ignoring tradition and dressing how they pleased. Francis Waring, vicar of Heybridge, Essex, from 1798 until his death in 1833, favoured a coat made from black and white yarns twisted together to give a speckled effect, black pantaloons, a bright yellow scarf and, even more incongrously, a tattered old straw hat. Most evenings he could be seen scurrying to the local pub with a large teapot, which, filled with beer, he would carry back to the vicarage for his supper.

The vicarage itself was sparsely furnished. Logs of wood served as chairs, and Waring and his plump wife slept in a wicker cradle on rockers. Where their children slept is not known, but they were brought up to feed from a wooden trough, like pigs, while their strange parents ate their meals in comparative luxury from crude earthenware dishes.

The Reverend Favell Hopkins, vicar of Bury, Huntingdonshire (1751-1788), was also an eccentric, noted for his meanness. Reluctant to spend money on new clothing, he wore the same garments every day until they became so threadbare that he was obliged to acquire a change. On one such occasion he was taking a walk along a country road when he spotted a scarecrow that was better dressed than he was, and shamelessly he exchanged clothing with it.

In 1813, the Reverend Joshua Waterhouse begrudgingly paid £2,000 to secure the rectory of Little Stukely, near Huntingdon, and was thereafter loathe to spend another penny on the building, even bricking up most of the windows to avoid paying window tax. He turned several of the rooms into granaries where he could store his corn until market prices rose. He paid such low wages to his workmen that eventually no-one would work for him, and his crops perished in the field. Shunned by the majority of his parishioners, he became almost a recluse, his main companions being the rats and mice that infested the filthy, neglected rectory.

On July 3, 1827, Waterhouse, then eighty one years old, was found dead in a brewing vat. He had been stabbed to death, and Joshua Slade, one of his former employees, was arrested and tried for murder at Huntingdon Assizes. After confessing that he had slaughtered the elderly vicar with a sword when he was disturbed, whilst attempting to rob him, Slade was found guilty and sentenced to death by hanging. He was executed on September 1, 1827.

The Reverend Thomas Archer, curate of Prittlewell, Essex, in the latter part of the 18th century, was a fanatical huntsman and wore his hunting clothes beneath his surplice so that he could dash off to join the local hunt immediately the service was over. If the sermon was running late for any reason, he was sometimes known to recite the benediction whilst hurrying down the aisle, discarding his surplice, and leaving the church before the congregation had risen from their knees. One thing Archer, a heavy smoker, never failed to do before leaving was to pick up his long clay pipe, which he placed ready-filled in a niche in the wall of the church near the vestry.

Another keen huntsman was the combative Bate Dudley. When he was curate of Bradwell church in Essex, he kept his own pack of hounds, and regularly engaged them in a hunt. A skilful horseman, Bate Dudley was fearless in his pursuit of his prey. On one occasion, after chasing the fleeing fox across treacherous countryside, he refused to be outwitted when the terrified creature clambered up the ivy-covered walls of Creeksea church and sought refuge on the roof of the chancel. The determined parson dismounted and climbed up the wall in pursuit, coaxing three pairs of hounds to follow him. Like him, they had no fear of danger when the scent of blood was so near. When they reached the top of the wall they tore the fox to pieces on the chancel roof.

Bate Dudley was an unusual clergyman who had several contrasting roles. In addition to his military and sporting interests, he was not only a lover of the theatre but jointly composed several comic operas with William Shield, a noted composer of the day. Although none were received enthusiastically by audiences, he became friendly with the Prince Regent, and the famous actor David Garrick.

As if all these activities were not enough, he plunged into the world of journalism and became editor of *The Morning Post* for a spell. The position obviously did not satisfy him, for in 1780 he founded his own newspaper, *The Morning Herald.*

James Hackman met actress Martha Ray long before he was ordained and was given the living of the parish of Wiveton, Norfolk, in March 1779, but the

The Reverend Sir Henry Bate Dudley, a keen huntsman, kept his own pack of hounds and, like them, was fearless in his pursuit of a fox.

appointment meant little to him as he had become infatuated with Martha and could think of nothing else but winning her love. Martha was the mistress of the Earl of Sandwich, and refused Hackman's frequent proposals of marriage until his infatuation turned into an insane jealousy.

Thinking that if he could not have her, no-one else would, he waited at the stage door of Covent Garden Theatre, where she was appearing, and when she left the stage, shot her dead. He then turned the pistol on himself, but was seized by members of the theatre staff before he could end his own life, and the pistol ball mearly grazed his head.

James Hackman was tried for murder, found guilty, and hanged at Tyburn on April 9, 1779. He was only twenty seven years old, and had been rector of Wiveton for forty days, but had never set foot in the parish.

Another clergyman who never visited his own parish was John Mavor, who, when curate of Foresthill, Oxfordshire, in 1825, was suddenly appointed Rector of Hadleigh, Essex. But Mavor had an ambition to open a college to prepare young men for ordination at Foresthill, and had no intention of moving to Hadleigh, so he engaged a curate to attend to his duties there.

No doubt he would have been better off had he moved to Hadleigh, for he borrowed a considerable sum of money to extend his Foresthill parsonage to accommodate students, but could not pay the loan back when only a few enrolled. Financial pressures made his tutorial sessions intolerable and his unpredictable moods drove away the few disgruntled students he had.

Without students, he had no hope of clearing his increasing debts, and was thrown into the debtors' prison at Oxford Castle. To recover the loan, the money-lenders were successful in having their own nominee appointed curate of Hadleigh, and received all the fees for weddings, funerals, and baptisms that were held at the church.

Ironically, Mavor became quite happy in prison, lecturing his fellow debtors. He even became unofficial prison chaplain, and was regularly visited by friends from Oxford colleges, who brought him a complete change of clothing at least once a year. He remained in the prison until he died of a stroke in 1853.

Many parsons, although also Justices of the Peace and, as such, administrators of the law, were not averse to turning a blind eye to illegal activities themselves, particularly if they had a chance of making personal gain. The numerous inlets and creeks round the East Anglian coast were ideal havens for smugglers, and nearby churches became the most suitable, and least suspected storage places for illicit cargo before it was transported inland.

The church at Great Bealing, near Woodbridge, was one such convenient place for the purpose, and the rector, Philip Meadows (1804-1837), had no qualms about assisting smugglers. He even allowed them use of his chaise to carry consignments of gin, brandy and tobacco inland. As the chaise was well-recognised in the vicinity as the rector's, it attracted no special attention.

Fritton Church in Suffolk was used by smugglers to store their contraband in an attic above the chancel, and several kegs of Hollands were once discovered beneath the altar of Theberton church.

Parson Woodford of Weston Longville had such a liking for spirits that he regularly purchased brandy, gin and rum from smugglers, on the cheap. Although he was never known to aid their illegal activities directly, he often recorded in his diary that a barrel of gin had been left outside the vicarage door during the night, and that he had spent the next morning bottling it.

Woodford had a scare one day in 1792 when he learned that excise officers had found a barrel of smuggled gin in the village blacksmith's house and were searching other domiciles under suspicion. The parson had a barrel of rum, which had been left for him the previous evening by Richard Andrews, whom he called 'the honest smuggler', for some obscure reason. Although Woodford became 'much agitated', his fears of exposure quickly diminished when the excise officers passed by, probably believing that a respectable clergymen was above suspicion.

The Sunday sermon was of course one of the most important items in a parson's weekly schedule and, whereas some had the knack of delivering a sharp, short sermon on any subject that occurred to them, others would spend most of the week preparing a long and monotonous diatribe that would have the congregation squirming in their seats. The Reverend John Fitzgerald (1803-1879), eldest brother of Edward Fitzgerald, who achieved lasting fame for his free translatiom of Omar Khayyam's *Rubaiyat*, was noted for his marathon sermons. He lived at Bougle Hall, near Woodbridge, and had a chapel built on to the house where he could hold services in his own unorthodox fashion.

In spite of his lengthy sermons, which usually embraced the evils of drink and slavery, his services were well-attended, mainly for their entertainment value, for the congregation were never sure what he would do next. Members sitting near the pulpit were accustomed to dodging hot wax as he waved a lighted candle at them to emphazise a point, but never knew when or why he would suddenly cease talking and begin whistling without explanation, then eventually resume his sermon as if such behaviour were normal.

But John Fitzgerald was anything but normal. When the chapel became uncomfortably hot in the summer, he would begin to strip while delivering his sermon. First he would remove his boots and stockings, then his outer garments, but always stopped, as one member of his congregation put it, 'before he exceeded the limits of decency'. Although some folk thought he was mad, particularly when they saw him regularly walking bare-footed around Woodbridge, with a tall hat tied to his head by a handkerchief, John Fitzgerald was a kindly man who meant well, but failed to inspire others because of his eccentricities.

The Reverend James Ford, rector of Naverstock, Essex, was a firm believer in punctuality and was known to become extremely agitated if anyone arrived at his church after the service had begun. He would glare at offenders for several minutes, as if they had committed a major sin. Unfortunately his wife was the biggest offender. Her late arrival in church became so regular, and Ford put up with it for so long, that one Sunday he could bear it no longer. When his wife crept into the church after the service had began, he halted proceedings, pointed an accusing finger at her, and bellowed: 'I wonder where you will be, madam, when the last trumpet sounds?' Whether this public humiliation made any difference to Mrs Ford's habitual lateness is not known.

Unpunctuality seems to have been the singular cause of incurring the Reverend Ford's wrath, but the Reverend William Layton, rector of St Matthew's, Ipswich (1775-1831), was known to become irritated by the slightest little thing that distracted him from whatever he was doing. The sound of a creaking door, for instance, would immediately send him scampering for oil, and a feather to apply it to the offending hinges, then forget about everything else until he had quelled the noise.

Apart from being upset by minor distractions, he was a fierce opponent of Sunday trading, and regularly condemned the practice from the pulpit. When he was walking through the streets of Ipswich one Sunday morning before the church service he came across a greengrocer selling fruit and vegetables from a stall in front of his shop. Ford became so infuriated at the sight of the trader's blatant disregard of the Sabbath that he kicked the supports of the stall away, then walked on, ignoring the shouts and curses of the greengrocer.

The angry trader, knowing that the parson ordered his Sunday dinner from a local baker, and condemning him as a hypocrite for supporting others who worked on Sundays, swore revenge. That same Sunday morning he lay in wait until the baker arrived at the rectory with the parson's dinner, then snatched the fine ribs of beef and the trimmings from the tray and threw the lot into the gutter. Satisfied that he had had his revenge, the greengrocer ran off chuckling, leaving the helpless baker to explain what had happened.

Disputes between parishioners and their resident parson were not uncommon, but although most were trivial and locally confined, a few developed into regional and even national scandals. In October 1844, the Reverend William Henslowe, rector of the parish of Wormgay, Norfolk, refused to conduct the funeral service, or have anything to do with the burial of a child named Sarah Bowden, because at the last minute he had discovered that she had been baptised by a Primitive Methodist minister. In spite of being ordered to proceed with the burial ceremony by the Bishop of Norwich, he adamantly refused to do so, but eventually allowed the parish clerk and churchwardens to conduct the ceremony and bury the child. Henslowe was eventually brought before an ecclesiastical court for disobeying the bishop, and was suspended from the ministry for three months.

A similar, but more heated, incident occurred in the hamlet of Akenfield, near Ipswich, in August 1878, when a child named Joseph Ramsey died unbaptised. When his distressed parents applied to have the body buried in the local graveyard, George Drury, the local vicar, aware that the parents were Baptists, said that he would allow the child to be buried in unconsecrated ground, reserved for still-born infants and suicides, and that no service was to be conducted within the churchyard.

George Drury, whose refusal to bury an unbaptised child caused the notorious Akenfield Burial Scandal.

On the day of the funeral, Drury, expecting to conduct a simple ceremony at the graveside, was astonished to see the funeral cortege halt at the churchyard gate. It was led by a dissenting minister named Wikham Tozer, who began reading passages of scripture. Drury interrupted him, and demanded that the party should proceed to the graveside, where they could perform whatever ceremony they wanted, but Tozer ignored him and continued reading. The rector became more agitated and kept interrupting Tozer until he calmly closed his bible and told him to keep quiet.

'I will not keep quiet,' Drury shouted, waving his umbrella. 'That child has not been baptised and is not a Christian. I object to it being buried as such.'

Tozer lost his patience, raised his fist threateningly and warned: 'I will soon silence your speech.'

'Don't shake your fist in my face,' yelled Drury. 'By God, you justly deserve to feel it!' Tozer retorted, but Drury backed away and said that if the coffin were not immediately conveyed to the grave he would lock the churchyard gates.

'Go to hell,' Tozer replied, opening his Bible,

and he resumed reading as though nothing had happened.

Drury locked the churchyard gates, then stormed off along the footpath to the rectory. When Tozer had finished his readings, the party broke through the hedge at the north end of the churchyard and lowered the little coffin containing the body of two year-old Joseph into its grave.

Although no reporter had been present to witness the shameful incident, a long, detailed account of it, in which Drury was portrayed as the villian, was published in a local newspaper. It was quickly seized upon and reprinted by national newspapers, and developed into a scandal. Drury, infuriated by the adverse publicity, particularly when he learned that Tozer had written the report, accused the editor of the local newspaper of libel and took him to court, claiming £2,000 damages.

Drury won the case, but was shocked when the judge decided that he should be awarded the paltry sum of forty shillings damages. However, the case untimately led to the passing of the Burial Law Reform Act of 1880, which stipulated that all Christians, of whatever faith, had the right to be buried in a churchyard.

An even greater scandal leading to an Act of Parliament occurred in the small village of Wetheringsett, near Stowmarket, in 1888. When rector John Sill died in 1883, the Bishop of Norwich appointed George Wilfred Ellis, the only candidate to apply for the position, to replace him. Ellis soon endeared himself to his parishioners, conducting baptisms, weddings and funerals with appropriate solemnity for five years, until 1888, when newcomers to the village recognised him, and exposed him as a fraud.

Investigations proved that he was not a registered clergyman and had never been ordained. He was arrested on charges of forging letters and falsely claiming to be in Holy Orders, found guilty at his trial, and sentenced to seven years' penal servitude in Dartmoor Prison. But that was not the end of the matter, for many villagers were faced with the fact that they were not legally married and that their children were illegitimate. Their concern was so great that it led to the Marriage Validation Act being passed by Parliament.

The Act contained a special clause which read: 'All marriages solemnised before the passing of this Act according to the rites of the Church of England, by the said George Wilfred Ellis, between persons believing him to have been duly ordained, shall be as valid as if the same had been solemnised before a duly ordained cleryman of the Church of England.'

When he was eventually discharged from prison Ellis set up a boarding house in London.

PRIVATEERS

VISIONS of a better life in a far land prompted thousands of English families to cross the Atlantic Ocean and settle in America, where the Pilgrim Fathers, having sailed from Plymouth in *The Mayflower*, in 1620, had founded a colony. Glowing accounts of the opportunities awaiting the adventurous, who were prepared to make the hazardous voyage across the Atlantic, influenced many East Anglians to emigrate and establish small colonies in what became known as New England.

They toiled long and hard to produce crops from the virgin soil, and built more and more permanent houses and developments until they became so numerous they formed new towns, which were named after the birthplaces of the first settlers – Norwich, Cambridge, Colchester, Sudbury, Harwich and Wymondham. Mass emigration to the New World continued for 150 years, but the settlers gradually became disillusioned and resented being controlled by the distant British government.

The colonists had no parliamentary representation and no say in the laws, taxes and trading restrictions the government imposed upon them. Resentment and increasing tension eventually boiled over into open rebellion, the first shots being fired in Lexington on April 19, 1775. The British government was not unduly concerned, believing that a rebellion of poorly-armed and ill-equipped farmers was a minor matter that would soon be quelled by the military. But they underestimated the strength of feeling and determination of the colonists to fight for their liberty.

Inflamed by such radical republicans as Thomas Paine, who had emigrated from Thetford, Norfolk, in 1774, the colonists declared war against Britain with the aim of gaining independence.

The colonists had no navy as such, but they converted merchant vessels, and any other suitable ships they could muster, into armed vessels, granting their owners Letters of Marque, and they deployed them far and wide to harass British shipping.

On the night of February 25, 1777, the Harwich packet, *Prince of Orange,* was returning from Holland when a cutter named *Surprise* drew alongside. The captain of the packet, fearing a collision, hailed his counterpart in good faith to alert him of the danger. Before he had time to question the motives of the *Surprise*, the armed crew of the American privateer leaped aboard and quickly overpowered him and his entire crew. Gustavus Cunningham, captain of the aptly named raider, triumphantly took command of the *Prince of Orange* and set sail for the French port of Dunkirk, where he planned to convert the vessel into an American privateer.

Dunkirk had long been used by pirates and privateers as a temporary base, but Cunningham saw it as an ideal port where an American fleet of privateers could be based under his command and easily sent to plunder or commandeer British ships. His success not only aroused the concern of the British Admiralty, who designated four frigates to patrol the English Channel and North Sea, but also caused embarrassment to the French government.

Although the French sympathised with the Americans, and openly supplied them with arms and munitions, they were averse to becoming actively involved in the conflict, and were particularly concerned when they discovered that Frenchmen were being recruited to crew the American privateers. Consequently, they arrested Cunningham and imprisoned him in Dunkirk, but Benjamin Franklyn, the American Commissioner in Paris, intervened and demanded that Cunningham and his compatriots be freed, on condition they left Dunkirk within twenty four hours and returned to America.

Their arrest, however, did not deter a considerable number of adventurous seamen from volunteering to man privateers, especially French nationals, and some English captives who were persuaded by the promise of a share in the profits, even at the risk of capture and execution as a traitor and pirate.

One of Cunningham's fleet, a large ship mounting twenty carriage guns, under the command of Lieutenant Reach, rather than return to America, as Cunningham had done, sailed for the Norfolk coast in search of plunder. A short distance from King's Lynn, Reach came upon a timber-laden ship which was easily captured. But Reach's idea of sailing his valuable prize to the nearest French port crumbled when the vessel ran into difficulties navigating the notorious sandbanks off Happisburgh. In danger of running aground, Reach was obliged to relinquish command of his prize and hand it back to its experienced crew, who safely manouvered it out of danger and sailed it into the port of Yarmouth.

British naval vessels were given authority to challenge every vessel that departed from a French port. This caused increasing friction between the British and French governments, and the situation came to a head in 1777 when France formally recognised the American Declaration of Independence and formed an alliance with the United States.

Britain immediately declared war on France, and had to face the French navy, as well as the increasing number of French and American privateers. Dunkirk merchants formed companies to buy ships, convert them into armed vessels and, after acquiring Letters of Marque, send them on marauding expeditions to plunder and capture British ships.

Even humble fishing vessels were not immune from attack by privateers. In November 1778 a fishing sloop, owned by Elias Loveday of Harwich, was attacked and captured by a French privateer named *Theresa*, under the command of Captain Jean Hossoia, who held the sloop and crew to ransom. The incident outraged the merchants of East Anglia, and they sent a letter of protest to the owners of the *Theresa* proposing that a pact be made between both nations to the effect that fishing vessels should be allowed to carry on their peaceful business with immunity.

The owners of the *Theresa* and other French merchants agreed. The crew of the British sloop were released, but the agreement proved of little value as ruthless privateers continued to attack every British vessel they spotted. In spite of the British Admiralty – which considered privateers to be nothing more than common pirates – deploying more frigates and cutters to hunt down and rid the seas of them, the number of privateers increased, and they became even more daring.

In March 1779 a navy cutter sighted a French privateer uncomfortably close to the north Norfolk coast and, suspecting that it might try to land in search of plunder, gave chase. When it was just off Cromer, the privateer suddenly opened fire, and a brisk but fierce battle ensued between the two vessels. So close to shore were they that several cannon balls fell near Cromer church. The privateer, her mast and sails considerably damaged, came off worse, but continued firing and managed to limp away and escape capture.

In July of the same year, the people of Dunwich, Suffolk, no doubt mindful of the incident at Cromer, became increasingly fearful that the crew of a French vessel, which had moored offshore, intended to land and plunder. They hid all their valuables, loaded carts with their possessions, and moved further inland, driving their cattle with them. Their fears were justified when an officer and twenty men from the vessel landed and searched the vacated village, only to find a few old fowl which were not worth taking. Foiled by the people of Dunwich, they returned to their ship empty-handed, without a shot being fired.

A cod smack sailing just off Southwold had a fortunate escape on the morning of August 9,1780, when what appeared to be a heavily-armed smuggling cutter gave chase with the obvious intention of capture. A few minutes later a fleet of large colliers came into view and the cutter veered away and fled. The cutter was not a smuggling vessel, but a 150 ton American privateer named

Fearnought, under the command of fearsome Captain Daniel Fall. The vessel was armed with eighteen four-pounder cannons, and was to terrorize the East coast for several months.

Fall furthered his rise to infamy on September 20, 1780, when he attacked a fleet of six British coal ships off Happisburgh and captured four of the smaller vessels without resistence. The two larger vessels, being armed, exchanged shots with *Fearnought*. After a fierce battle one was obliged to surrender, but the other succeeded in beating off the attacker and fled. Over the next few weeks Fall captured thirty ships, all of which he held to ransom for amounts ranging from 300 to 700 guineas. The majority of the owners of the seized vessels, rather than suffer loss of trade, paid up, and Fall quickly accummulated a fortune.

Flushed with success, and spurred on by the ease of capturing vessels without encountering much resistance, he became even more daring. On January 31, 1781, a large brigantine, named *Alexander and Margaret*, set off from North Shields laden with coal. When she was just off Cromer she was suddenly attacked by Fall's *Fearnought*. Although the brigantine, under the command of Captain David Bartleman, was equipped with only four eight-pounder cannons, a fierce battle ensued, which lasted two hours.

At one point, Bartleman managed to beat off *Fearnought*, but Fall returned and attacked the brigantine with such ferocity that Bartleman, his first mate killed, all the crew injured, and seriously wounded himself, was forced to surrender and pay Fall 400 guineas ransom. When released, his battered crew courageously managed to sail the stricken ship into Yarmouth port, but Bartleman died shortly afterwards as a result of his extensive wounds and was buried in the churchyard of St Nicholas, Yarmouth.

Fall was becoming such a menace that merchants and ship owners along the East Coast expressed concern that little was being done to stop him seizing their vessels. Timothy Stewart, commander of a Yarmouth privateer named *Dreadnought*, wanted to raise a fleet of armed ships, solely for the purpose of tracking and intercepting Fall's *Fearnought*, and blast it to pieces. But such was Fall's awesome reputation that no-one would join Stewart in his proposed venture.

Consequently, Fall continued marauding and became even more adventurous. On the night of June 14, 1781, accompanied by another privateer, named *Liberty*, he chased the Harwich packet, *Prince of Wales*, for three hours until worn down by ceaseless bombardment, the packet's captain surrendered after throwing the mail bags overboard so that any government mail would not find its way into enemy hands.

The captain of the packet and his crew were handcuffed and transferred onto the *Liberty,* which set sail for the Dutch port of Flushing. While entering Flushing Haven *Liberty* ran aground on a sandbank and became stuck fast. Fortunately *Fearnought* was close by and was able to rescue the crew and prisoners and carry them safely into Flushing. There the crew of the packet were held to ransom.

Fall's reign of terror began to decline in September 1781, when he attacked a small convoy of ships and their escort vessel, the *Monkey*, a Yarmouth revenue cutter. The *Monkey*, under the command of Captain Glasspoole, put up such fierce resistance that Fall was beaten off after only a brief engagement, and fled. When the cutter returned to Yarmouth, Captain Glasspoole was presented with a silver plate at a public reception in recognition of his achievement in thwarting the dreaded Fall. Two months later, *Fearnought* was spotted in the North Sea by HMS *Albermarle*, which chased the privateer for about an hour until it disappeared from view.

Whether Fall found out later that HMS *Albermarle* was under the command of Horatio Nelson is not known, but, although he continued his activities around the Scottish coast and the Irish Sea, he was never seen again along the East Anglian coast, no doubt concluding that he could no longer capture ships with ease.

His departure did not deter other privateers from attempting to seize British vessels plying off the East Coast, in spite of the increased risk of capture. The captains of some captured privateers, although claiming to be American citizens carrying Letters of Marque issued by the French Admiralty, were suspected of being Englishmen and were brought to trial, accused of the capital offence of piracy, as were English members of their crew. Those found guilty were condemned as traitors and hanged.

William Payne was the captain of a small privateer named *Cerf-Volant,* which was pursued down the East Anglian coast in April 1781 by the revenue cutter *Liberty* until it was forced ashore near Southwold. Payne gave orders to abandon ship, and fled inland on foot, as did the crew. John Allen, master of the *Liberty,* landed his vessel shortly afterwards and, with a party of his men, set off in search. The majority of the *Cerf-Volant's* crew were quickly rounded-up, and Payne was found comfortably seated by the fireside in a country inn, calmly smoking his pipe. When challenged, he produced Letters of Marque issued by the High Admiral of France, appointing him commander of the *Cerf-Volant*, and he claimed to be an American citizen born in Boston, New England.

But John Allen knew that Payne had at one time been master of a Yarmouth vessel, and he was arrested and first taken to Yarmouth gaol, as were the captured members of his crew, then transferred to Newgate gaol to await trial at the Admiralty Sessions at the Old Bailey. His persistent claim that he was an American citizen was shattered when John Boulter, from Northrepps, Norfolk, was called. Boulter swore that he had known the accused since childhood and remembered him living in the parish of Northrepps with his parents.

Parish registers were produced, and the entry, 'William, son of Richard and Elizabeth Payne, born 23rd April, 1738,' was enough to convince the jury that Payne was an Englishman, guilty of treachery, and piracy. He was sentenced to death and was hanged on November 28, 1781. His body was transported to Yarmouth, where it swung from a gibbet on the South Denes as a warning to would-be pirates until 1804.

Apart from claiming to be American citizens, some Englishmen, who willingly helped man enemy privateers, tried whatever means they could think of to avoid the gallows. Joseph Evans, for instance, one of several English members of the crew of the privateer *L'Escamateur* – a large heavily-armed cutter, which had captured the sloop *Nottingham* off Cromer in September 1782 and was sailing for Dunkirk with her prize – must have realized that eventual surrender was inevitable when HMS *Fly*, cruising off Mundesley, gave chase.

But the privateer put up such fierce resistance that Thomas Roberts, her American captain, refused to capitulate for five hours until the British naval cutter *Hunter* joined in the battle. The defeated *L'Escamateur* was escorted to Yarmouth with the re-possessed *Nottingham*. Captain Roberts proved himself to be a genuine American citizen, but Joseph Evans, perhaps unlucky enough to be singled out from the English members of the crew, was charged with piracy. At his trial, Evans claimed that he was a prisoner on board the *L'Escamateur* and had been forced to help man the ship, but several witnesses for the prosecution testified to the contrary, and claimed that they knew him as a barber in Woodbridge, Suffolk. It took the jury just fifteen minutes to find him guilty of piracy, and he was sentenced to death.

Thomas Roberts, having proved that he was an American citizen carrying Letters of Marque issued by the French Admiralty, was sentenced to imprisonment. He suffered the unhealthy conditions prevalent in Yarmouth gaol until January 1783 when, having broken free from his irons, he suddenly attacked the gaoler's daughter when she brought him food, and seized the keys of the cell from her. But, trained to deal with rebellious prisoners, the girl fought back, grabbed hold of his clothing and called for assistance. The response was immediate, and Roberts was quickly secured back in his cell.

Although Roberts' attempt to escape was foiled, it was discovered that it had been planned with outside help, and that he had several sympathizers who were willing to shelter him in their homes on the route to a safe town. As a consequence, Roberts was transferred to Newgate prison.

British shipowners and the crews of their vessels rejoiced in 1783 when the war with France and the United States was ended by all parties signing the Treaty of Versailles. This stipulated that England agreed to recognise the independence of the United States of America and return colonies in India to France. The peace lasted for ten years until war broke out between Britain and the newly-created French Republic in 1793.

Once again, French ports along the English Channel became bases for French privateers. Not only were British ships constantly under fear of sudden attack, but the threat of invasion of England by the French caused much concern, particularly when military genius Napoleon Bonaparte became Emperor of France in 1804.

Privateers were, of course, interested only in financial gain, and made the most of the opportunity during the long war between England and France by lurking in the numerous shallow creeks and estuaries of Suffolk and Essex so that they could make sudden attacks on unsuspecting British vessels. The East Coast was notorious for its treacherous hidden sandbanks, which made navigation difficult and sometimes disastrous for those unfamiliar with safe shipping routes. Privateers would often gather in the safe waters of Yarmouth Roads waiting for the cod and herring fleets to return to port with their catch.

Such was the menace that the Admiralty stationed a sloop at Yarmouth, shortly after the war began, to protect the fishing fleets but, as most privateers were armed, it was frequently engaged in sea battles around the East Coast and in the English Channel.

The ingenuity of a cabin boy on the Scottish brig *Snow Enterprise*, saved it and its cargo of coal, from being taken to a French port when it was captured off the East Coast by a French privateer named *La Venguer* in 1797. With the exception of the cabin boy, the captain of the privateer imprisoned all the crew of the brig in his own vessel and replaced them with seven of his own crew to take his valuable prize into the port of Dunkirk.

Considered harmless, the cabin boy had free run of his ship, and he seized an opportunity to drive a nail into the compass so that it would malfunction. The French seaman who had been given the responsibility of navigating the captured brig, relied solely on the compass for guidance, and believed the vessel was nearing Dunkirk, when it was only just off Cromer. He instructed the cabin boy to hoist a signal flag for a pilot to guide them into port, but the lad hoisted a flag signalling distress instead. A small fishing boat nearby, seeing the distress signal, drew alongside and the cabin boy shouted that the brig had been captured by the French. The fishing boat immediately returned to Cromer and gave the alarm.

Two armed vessels, manned by the Cromer Volunteers, instantly put to sea

Privateers and the Navy do battle near Wells.

to recapture the *Snow Enterprise* but, realizing he had been fooled, the seaman in temporary charge of the brig set sail and followed the now distant privateer, which was armed with a single swivel-gun. The chase lasted for eight hours, but the Cromer Volunteers encountered little resistance and eventually recaptured the brig and brought it safely into the port of Yarmouth. The French crew were marched off to gaol. What happened to the heroic cabin boy, whose name is unknown, and whether he received due recognition for services beyond the call of duty is not recorded.

In July of the same year a French privateer, mounted with twelve large guns, attacked six vessels off Wells. After sinking one and setting fire to another, it captured the other four. The inhabitants of Wells, hearing heavy gunfire at sea and seeing a vessel ablaze close to shore, feared the French were going to land and plunder the town, but the privateer sailed away, content with its four captured vessels.

The menace of French privateers was rapidly becoming so serious that British vessels sailing off the East Coast frequently had to run the gauntlet before they reached the safety of a port. Spurred on by their successes, the French became more daring, sometimes to the point of recklessness, in spite of their losses. A few days after the incident off Wells, the British revenue cutter *Viper* spotted a privateer named *Graces* lurking in the shallows of the River Swallet. After a brief encounter, the cutter captured the privateer. The following month it captured the *Espour,* which was lying in the mouth of the River Naze. Between 1797 and 1807, several privateers were captured, twelve off the port of Yarmouth, the most notorious of which was the *La Contre-Amiral Magon* under the command of corsair Jean Blanckman.

Blanckman had terrorised the seas around the East Coast for so long that British seamen breathed a sigh of relief when his reign came to an end. Although his vessel was equipped with seventeen guns, Blanckman seldom had to fire them as his ship was painted in the fashion of a fishing vessel, and the members of his crew could be seen on deck dressed as fishermen. When drawing alongside an unsuspecting vessel he would ask the captain if he required any fish. This was the verbal signal for members of his crew to appear from below deck, clamber aboard the other vessel and seize it. He made numerous captures in this piratical way and considerably enriched himself and his crew.

But in November 1804, Captain Hancock, in command of the British sloop HMS *Cruizer,* became suspicious when he spotted Blanckman's 'fishing' vessel calmly sailing off the Belgian port of Ostend. His suspicions increased, and he immediately gave chase when Blanckman ignored a signalled request to identify and made off. The chase continued all night, but the wind freshened early the following morning, catching Blanckman unawares. His vessel lost its topsail and, out of control, ran aground.

Hancock captured it without firing a shot and, being familiar with tides and conditions around the Belgian shores, brought the privateer brig safely across the North Sea and beached her at Yarmouth. Blanckman and his crew of ninety five were temporarily locked up in Yarmouth gaol. The crew were later escorted by the militia to the prisoner of war camp at Norman Cross, and Blanckman was taken to a prison ship at Chatham. His privateering days were over. The crew of HMS *Cruizer* were each rewarded with £26 for their part in capturing this most feared corsair.

In September 1807 the brig *Endeavour* was attacked off the Essex coast by the French privateer *L'Etoile*, a large vessel mounting fourteen guns, which transferred a few members of its crew on to the brig after capturing it to ensure that it would be taken to Dunkirk. Shortly after this incident the revenue cutter *Argus,* alarmed by gunfire, came on to the scene and attempted to retake *Endeavour* by opening fire on *L'Etoile*. In the ensuing battle the vessels came so close that they collided.

Realizing their vessel had been badly holed and was sinking, the French jumped aboard the *Argus*, engaged in hand-to-hand fighting and quickly took over command. They sailed her into Dunkirk, leaving their own vessel to settle in its grave at the bottom of the sea. The surviving crew of the *Argus* were marched off to gaols at Arras and Givet; five had been killed in the battle. As four of their own crew had been killed, and their vessel lost for ever, the *L'Etoile* crew had little sympathy for their captives who had to struggle to survive in the harsh conditions of French prisons.

But the French cannot be condemned for engaging ruthless privateers, for Britain had no qualms about giving licence to their own during the long war. One notable British privateer was the schooner *Courier,* captained by George Munnings, who had previously been the commander of a revenue cutter. Munnings armed the 150 ton schooner, and fitted it with six six-pound carronade carriage guns.

A red-headed, hot-tempered man, he had no trouble in making the thirty four crew members he engaged sign an agreement that they would each receive one guinea for every successful capture accomplished and make no further claim to any part of it. He had many successes by plundering French ships in the North Sea, until the war with France ended in 1815, and all vessels were able to navigate the North Sea and English Channel without fear of sudden attack by licenced terrorists, which is what all peace-loving seamen considered them to be.

Although privateers continued to operate in seas surrounding other countries when a war broke out, most maritime nations ceased issuing Letters of Marque by signing the Declaration of Paris in 1856. This stipulated that the captain and crew of any unofficially-armed vessel attacking another vessel would be committing piracy, and would be breaching maritime law. Thus the long reign of the privateers ended.

THE SEARCH FOR TRUE LOVE

A LTHOUGH February 14 has been celebrated as St Valentine's Day for centuries, the practice of sending love tokens on that day has no connection with a particular individual named Valentine.

Valentine is, in fact, the name of several saints, none of whom fits the legendary picture of the romantic paramour portrayed in fiction. Two of these martyred saints, Valentine of Rome, a priest, and Bishop Valentine of Terni, were beheaded on the same day, February 14, c270, during the reign of the Roman Emperor Claudius II, who disapproved of their Christian faith.

The date of the executions coincided with preparations for the Roman festival of Lupercalia on February 15, when various rituals were performed in honour of the Roman god Lupercus, one of which was a lottery, whereby boys drew the name of girls to partner them in the festivities. It seems plausable that this part of the Roman festival became merged with the patronal feast day of St Valentine when the Romans were converted to Christianity, and that St Valentine's Day has been celebrated romantically, perhaps more than religiously, on February 14 ever since.

Margery Drew was serious enough when she wrote a letter to John Paston III of Norwich in 1477. She carefully penned: 'My heart me bids ever more to love you truly over all earthly things.' John must have been a good catch because Margery's mother, Dame Elizabeth Drew, supported her letter with one of her own inviting him to come and stay at their dwelling on February 14, adding: 'Friday is St Valentine's Day and every bird chooses for himself a mate'. The combined efforts of mother and daughter had the desired effect. John took up the invitation and he and Margery were married later that year.

If a fenland lass were unsuccessful in securing a sweetheart on St Valentine's Day, and was frightened of being left on the shelf, she probably waited impatiently until February 24, St Martin's Eve, when custom required her to sow hemp seed in her garden at midnight whilst chanting the following:

Hemp seed I sow,
Hemp seed grow;
He that is my true love
Come after me and mow.

A young woman performing such a ritual today would probably be arrested for growing cannabis, which is the botanical name for hemp, but it was widely cultivated for the manufacture of rope and linen in the past, and anyone could grow it without breaking the law.

The quest for a soul-mate, of course, went on all the year round, not only by anxious spinsters but also by bachelors who must have felt their chances were running out. Not many of them were as particular in their requirements as a fellow calling himself Mr Sembre Contento, who advertised in an 1829 edition of the *Cambridge Chronicle* for 'Any single lady who is of a respectable family and has received a good education, who is not too young, too handsome, nor too rich, and not the contrary to the above qualifications'.

He went on to suggest a meeting during the day at a public place in Cambridge, and required any lady who considered herself suitable to describe the attire she would be wearing in a post-paid letter to the Cambridge Post Office. Whether the anonymous gentleman ever received a reply is not known, as he stressed the need for great secrecy.

Thomas Sadler of Ipswich, who tried his hand at verse in an endeavour to gain a wife, had no qualms about seeing it printed in full in the *Ipswich Journal*. It read:

> *Address To The Suffolk Females:*
> *Wanted immediately as a wife*
> *And partner throughout life,*
> *One that is in temper mild —*
> *As meek and gentle as a child;*
> *One that's healthy, young, and strong,*
> *And will not vex me with her tongue;*
> *One that's not o'er nice in dress,*
> *No more than humble cleanliness;*
> *One that's not o'erwhelmed with care,*
> *Nor e'er will drive me to despair;*
> *One that won't abroad be straying,*
> *Nor know no bed but what we lay in,*
> *One that's not o'erwhelmed with riches,*
> *Nor e'er will want to wear the breeches,*
> *But with me, in my humble state,*
> *Strive to be happy, in whatever fate*
> *May on us fall in this short life,*
> *Meanwhile that we are man and wife;*
> *For swift the hours of pleasure fly*
> *When love's entwined with constancy;*

But when once sullied by a jealous strife,
Slow moves the hour of bitter life.
A virtuous wife is an honour to her birth;
A discontented wife is a hell on earth.
Now any lass whose will incline,
And wish to know where she may find
The man who is so much inclined
To enter in this happy state,
I my abode will now relate.
I am a native of Ipswich town,
My name in here I won't put down,
But if to find me out you are inclined,
Come over Stoke, and there you will me find,
In a house where I was born and bred,
Well nigh unto the Boar's Head.

The following reply appeared in the same newspaper a week later:

Address To The Suffolk Bachelor:
Sir,
A young lady from Norfolk has read your petition
And is highly concerned at your woeful condition,
But the reason for that you yourself have betrayed,
Your head is too nigh a Boar's Head, I'm afraid;
And so, if from Suffolk you look for a wife,
Get away from that hog for the rest of your life,
For what Suffolk female, though ever so poor,
Wold look for a husband so nigh to a Boar?'

This was obviously not the kind of reply Thomas Sadler expected, but one that could have induced him to seek temporary solace in the Boar's Head Inn, if only to improve his efforts to write inspiring poetry.

But even when a single person of either sex was successful in gaining a sweetheart, by whatever means, courtship often brought disappointments and sometimes shocks. Like that befalling a young man who was proudly walking his newly-found sweetheart to Stirbitch Fair in Cambridge on a windy day in September 1770. Her much-admired French curls suddenly flew from her head on a gust of wind, leaving her totally bald pate exposed. The fellow immediately let go of her arm and stood and stared at her in disbelief as she burst into tears and tried to cover her head in shame.

A young man named Dewey from Littleport, who was happily courting farmer Dent's buxom young daughter, had no idea that her miserly father, whilst welcoming a prospective son-in-law to his house, was keeping a record of all the food and drink he consumed during his visits. When a proposal of marriage seemed imminent, farmer Dent presented a bill to young Dewey for £1 12s 6d, itemising five breakfasts, twenty six teas and seven dinners provided for him on his visits. Whether the amount included a service charge is not known, but the bill certainly put an end to the romance, and a Dewey-Dent marriage never took place.

Fenland fathers who were anxious to get an eligible spinster daughter off their hands sometimes resorted to what was known as 'bundling'. The front door would be left open, or a ladder conveniently placed against the daughter's bedroom window at night as a silent invitation to any young man willing to court her. The custom is mentioned in the last two verses of an old Fenland song, recalled by writer WH Barrett. They include some of the pitfalls a venturesome lover should consider before taking the plunge:

> *Nip into bed and snuggle down*
> *Beside the warm body in a nightgown.*
> *If her sister is there then rise in a stew;*
> *You can bundle with one but not with two.*
>
> *Now, lusty lads, just listen to me:*
> *A bundle's a bundle wherever it be.*
> *There's only one ending for me to sing:*
> *The parson won't bless you as he puts on the ring.*

Of course, not all parents, particularly fathers, were anxious to get their offspring off their hands, and did everything in their power to prevent or end a courtship. A young man from Royston, with the unusual name of Beach Wood, was heartbroken when his domineering father took a dislike to the girl he was courting and forbade him to ever see her again. Young Beach was so distraught that he did nothing but pine away for a lost love. He died of a broken heart at the age of twenty five and was buried on July 4, 1744. His gravestone bore the following inscription:

> *Beneath this peaceful stone here lies*
> *To cruel love a sacrifice;*
> *But reader mind the youth was slain*
> *By papa's, not the girl's disdain,*
> *For when the lover went to woo,*
> *The maid said yes, the father no,*
> *So through mere rage, to be denied,*
> *He broke his heart, and so he died.*
> *Young men take care, lest you have to grieve,*
> *Nor damsels court without your parents' leave.*

In spite of parental opposition, other couples were not so easily denied a union. When George Cooper of West Stow, Suffolk, was forbidden to court Elizabeth Steel by her folk, and discovered she was locked in her bedroom, he waited until dark, then procured a ladder from a nearby barn, gained entry to her room and carried her down to a waiting carriage. They sped through the night to Gretna Green and were married by the blacksmith on February 17, 1816.

The length of a courtship varied considerably according to circumstances. Perhaps the shortest courtship on record was that between Arthur Barrow and Martha Edwards, both of Stapleford, Cambridge. Arthur, a gamekeeper, spotted the widowed Martha and considered she was fair game on March 23, 1792. After wooing her for a mere two hours twenty five minutes, he rushed her to the altar and they were married the same day.

Other couples were less hasty to commit themselves. William Nunn finally married Sarah Twitchett at Bury St Edmunds on March 14, 1793 after courting her for twenty five years. But that was a brief span of time compared to the courtship of John Bacon of Saffron Walden and his lady-love, which lasted forty years. They were both sixty years-old when at last they decided to wed on February 9, 1818.

In those days, as now, a considerable age gap between couples was no barrier to a marriage, and such weddings caused much interest and speculation as to the underlying motives of the younger partner. A large crowd assembled at Fakenham church on August 25, 1829, to witness the marriage of seventy nine year-old Thomas Hubbard and his twenty one year-old bride, Martha Frary. Thomas hobbled into the church with his ninety year-old best man, and they took turns supporting each other whilst awaiting the officiating clergyman, who was late arriving. After the delayed ceremony, Thomas was lifted into an open carriage beside his young wife and they were drawn through the main streets of the town to the accompaniment of gunfire and shouts of the crowds. What they shouted is best left to the imagination!

Some widows could not come to terms with their lonely state and shamelessly went all out to seek a second husband. In 1852, which was a leap year, Jemima Turner of Swaffham Prior set her sights on a thirty seven year-old bachelor named William Hancock, who reluctantly agreed to marry her after she had determinedly broken his resistance. On the day of the wedding, the bridegroom failed to turn up at the parish church.

Unlike many brides who would have burst into tears, Jemima had the whole village searched and William was eventually found going about his normal daily tasks. When reminded that it was his wedding day he openly admitted that he 'had forgot it'. After receiving a humiliating verbal thrashing in public by Jemima, William was practically forced to go through with the wedding the following morning, when about 100 women and children, some rendering a discordant version of 'Haste to the Wedding' on improvised instruments, escorted him along the streets of the village to the church. Satisfied that she had at last legally bound her man, the forceful Jemima agreed with William that guests should be encouraged to celebrate the occasion well into the small hours. When they had all departed, she retired to the bridal chamber and waited for her captured husband to join her.

The longer she waited the more frustrated she became. Then frustration turned to anger when a friend came and told her that William had 'betook himself off'. For the second time in two days, Jemima had the entire village searched, but William could not be found, and never was. Where he went to and what happened to him remains a mystery.

An unusual and possibly unique hitch occurred at a wedding between Sarah Newell and Arthur Wilson at Hatfield Broadoak parish church when the local vicar became indisposed and asked in the Reverend Walter Hiley to officiate in his place. Mr Hiley was unfamiliar with the church and knew few of the congregation, least of all the bride and groom. He must have had his mind fixed on anything other than the sacred ceremony he was conducting, because he married the bride to the best man, who happened to be her brother, Abraham!

Bride, bridegroom and best man must have either been drunk or stupid, because while Abraham obediently slipped the ring on his sister's finger, Arthur calmly stood by watching the procedure in silence. Incredibly, no-one realised that brother and sister had been declared man and wife until they were about to sign the register. The stand-in clergyman suddenly became aware that something was seriously wrong and halted the proceedings, but had no idea how to rectify his mistake. Panic-stricken, he sent for the resident vicar to help him sort out the blunder.

None too pleased at being called from his other engagement, the local vicar was obliged to attend his church and declare the marriage null and void. Arthur and Sarah were then legally joined together in a second ceremony. But having gone through such a trauma at their wedding it is unknown if the couple lived happily ever after or put in a claim for the renowned Dunmow Flitch.

The custom of presenting a flitch of bacon to the married couple who could give satisfactory proof that they had lived together in perfect harmony for a year and a day, and had never once regretted marrying, originated in the 13th century. The flitch was offered annually by the Manor of Dunmow, Essex, and the applicants were required to prove their claim to a jury whilst kneeling on

Winners of the Dunmow Flitch are cheered by the crowds.

two sharp stones near the door of the church. Needless to say, only a few instances of the flitch being claimed have been recorded over the centuries.

One such couple who successfully passed the stringent trial, which was conducted by a jury of five women, in 1701, were John and Ann Reynolds. Having undergone the ordeal, they must have wondered whether it had been worth it when they were presented with a gammon of bacon instead of a flitch – a gammon being only the thigh of a pig, whereas a flitch is a whole side.

No other claiments were recorded until 1751, when Thomas and Ann Skakeshaft travelled from Wethersfield, Suffolk, to face a jury of six bachelors and six spinsters, and managed to convince them that they had lived together in wedded bliss for seven years. They, too, were awarded a gammon of bacon instead of a flitch, but instead of complaining made the most of being cheated by selling portions of it to the crowds, who had come from near and far to witness the event, and made a considerable profit.

A couple who never stood a chance of being awarded even a slice of bacon, in Dunmow or anywhere else, were a Mr and Mrs Hanson from Padstow. They married on a Tuesday in November 1816, but had 'grown sullen towards each other' by the following day. On Thursday they stopped speaking to each other, but the strained silence and tense domestic atmosphere erupted into an almighty row on Friday. Sadly, the only time they ever saw eye to eye on anything was on the Saturday when they agreed that the marriage would never work, and decided on a permanent seperation.

Some men, probably gluttons for punishment, illegally acquired two or more wives, but usually managed to keep their divided matrimonial affairs secret. Edmund Mallett of Acle, Norfolk, must have been desperate for cash when he was arrested for horse stealing in October 1768. The fact that he had four wives and several children by each wife to support, all living in different locations and none being aware that the others existed, failed to impress the jury when he was brought to trial on the charge of horse-stealing at Wisbech Assizes. Although bigamy was confirmed as a felony by Act of Parliament in 1603, it was not classed as a capital offence, whereas horse-stealing was, and Edmund ended his days on the gallows for the comparatively minor felony of stealing a horse.

Not long after John Mason of Thetford married Frances Duffield at Hardingham on September 21, 1818, he was accused of already having a wife and was brought to trial for bigamy at the Thetford Spring Assizes. Several witnesses gave evidence against him, and the parish register proved that he had married Mary Ann Suffield five years previously. He was found guilty of committing bigamy and was sentenced to transportation to Australia for twelve years. Transportation almost invariably turned out to be a life sentence, as very few ever made the return journey when their sentences were completed. John probably settled to a life down under and may eventually have found himself another wife or two.

Before the Matrimonial Clauses Act was passed by Parliament in 1857, once a couple had wed, the chances of them obtaining a divorce or a legal separation if the marriage failed were stacked against them. It was possible for one partner to sue the other in the church courts on the grounds of adultery or life-threatening cruelty, and plead for a legal separation, but this excluded permission to re-marry, and the procedure was so costly that only the rich and influential could afford it.

A divorce could be granted only by an Act of Parliament, and the expense was far beyond the means of the majority of disillusioned marital misfits. Not surprisingly desertion was a common law-breaking offence, and local authorities went to great lengths to bring an errant spouse of either sex to justice to avoid having to support their dependants on parish funds.

In March 1779 the authorities in Littleport, Cambridgeshire, were moved to place a detailed description in the local newspaper of each of the six men who deserted their families during that month. It read as follows:

'. . . *JOHN SPARROW, a labourer about 26 years of age, about 5' 6" high, broad set, florid complexion, dark lank hair, Roman nose, walks rather wide and turns his toes a little inward.*

'Also JOHN ELLINGHAM, a carpenter or sawyer, about 25 years of age, about 5' 6" high, a thin man, with ruddy complexion, dark lank hair, Roman nose, and a little knap-kneed.

'Also JOHN NICHOLAS, a labourer, about 23 years of age, and about 5' 6" high, broad set and round-shouldered, light coloured hair rather inclined to curl, fresh complexion, Roman nose, light grey eyes, and walks stooping and wide.

'Also THOMAS CRABB, a waterman or labourer, about 24 years of age and about 5' 1" high, with a dark complexion, short dark curled hair, dark eyes, a dimple in his chin, and walks upright and strutting.

'Also JOHN CLARK, a labourer, about 28 years of age, and about 5' 4" high, with a fresh complexion, dark lank hair, and an inpediment in his speech.

'Also THOMAS FISH, a wagoner or labourer, about 26 years of age, and about 5' 6" high, rather fresh in complexion, with brown hair, is well made and walks clean.'

It is interesting to note that, apart from nearly all the runaways having some form of physical defect, three had Roman noses, four were named John, two Thomas, and all were in their twenties and of similar height.

Statistics prove little, but the six had more in common than an unhappy marriage, and it is easy to imagine them getting together to plot an escape from their responsibilities. Whether that were so, or the high number of desertions in such a short space of time in the small community of Littleport was mere coincidence is not known, but, in spite of a reward of two guineas a man being offered for information that would lead to the apprehension of each of them, there is no record of any of them being caught.

William Trudgett of Great Shelford was not so fortunate. After leaving his wife and family, who were obliged to live on the poor rate for six months, he was arrested in November 1816 and charged with desertion. Brought to trial, William pleaded not guilty, stating that he had merely gone in search of work and had sent home as much money as he could afford, but was unable to prove that he had done so. The Bench was not impressed by his claims or intentions and committed him to gaol for one month as a warning.

When John Taylor's wife, Ann, left their home in Stoke-by-Nayland on March 3, 1775 to live with another man, John was quick to disclaim responsibility for any debts she might incur by publishing a warning to all persons that she was not to be trusted. Oddly enough, he added a rider to the effect that if she returned home immediately she would be 'kindly received'.

It is unlikely that Mary Botterwright of Fressingfield, Suffolk, would have been welcomed back by her husband, Jonathan, after she ran off with an excise officer named Carter in June 1783. Not content with taking £500 of Jonathan's money, she also took his pocket watch, all the buckles from his shoes and most of his clothes – and she managed to obtain considerable sums of money from his debtors by forging receipts in his name.

Jonathan must have had more cash stashed away, however, otherwise he would not have been able to promise 'to reward handsomely' any person who could give information as to Mary's whereabouts.

John Green, who sold his wife for a barrel of beer at King's Lynn market.

Liability for debts incurred by a runaway wife was a major problem for a deserted husband. One way to free himself from financial obligations was to obtain a separation by written deed, but the cost was beyond the reach of the poor. Their main alternative was to conduct what became known as a public divorce. This took the form of a wife sale, generally by public auction in the market square. Although recognised by the lower classes as a valid method of divorce, wife-selling was not sanctioned by law, and was generally frowned upon as a defiance of moral and legal obligations, as well as being a vulgar and degrading exhibition.

When John Green was sacked from his job at the Duke's Head Inn in King's Lynn, he set up as the tavern shoe-black, but took to heavy-drinking and gambling at the same time. Needless to say he soon found himself in financial difficulties, so decided to sell his wife. He first placed a halter round the submissive woman's neck, then led her to Lynn market place, where he invited the astounded crowds to make bids for her. The unfortunate woman must have been physically unattractive because the only offer he received in exchange for her was a gallon of beer, which he readily accepted.

Samuel Balls, of Blythburgh, had no difficulty in selling his wife to Abraham Rade for one shilling in 1789 but, to ensure he was free from marital obligations, he published a notice disclaiming responsibility for her, which read: 'No person or persons to entrust her with my name, for she is no longer my right'.

A large crowd gathered in Cambridge market place in December 1789 when Richard Hawkins tied a cord to his wife's waist, and led her around the busy market place, offering her for sale. Eventually he agreed to sell her to a stonemason named William Gibbs for five shillings. Gibbs explained that he had only three shillings on him, but promised to pay the balance as soon as possible if Hawkins would allow him credit. Hawkins agreed and handed the cord to Gibbs. The bartered wife was so pleased with her new husband that she gave him a kiss, but insisted that he bought her another wedding ring. Gibbs promised that he would, and the two happily walked away arm-in-arm, leaving the crowd gaping at them in amazement.

A farmer from Stowupland, Suffolk, was so delighted with the deal when he sold his wife to a neighbour for five guineas that he gave her a guinea as a parting gift so that she could buy herself a new dress. He then went to the parish church and requested that the bells be rung to celebrate such a satisfactory end to his marriage.

A Mr Stebbings from Norwich thought he had made a good deal when he sold his wife for £6 10s to a man named Turner, in 1823, and took up with a more favourable wife – until things went wrong. Having paid £4 down on his newly-acquired wife, Turner took her home and immediately turned his lawful spouse out of the house. When the now-destitute original Mrs Turner applied to the authorities for poor relief, they were not satisfied with her story and ordered both husbands to appear before the Mayor of Norwich with the women they claimed to be their rightful wives, and undergo investigations as to their legal marital position.

After listening to their individual versions at length, the bewildered Mayor finally ordered each husband to take only his original and legal wife back into her rightful home and support her. The unhappy four were subjected to a hustling from a jeering crowd who had gathered outside the Town Hall, and they had difficulty in making their way to resume what must have been anything but a life of bliss.

Whether Stebbings ever returned the £4 down-payment on the agreed credit sale of his wife to Turner is not recorded.